Debug Your Brain
bret carr

dedicated to you who are perching on the ledge
and are about to learn that upon jumping,
your wings will be there -
if you simply
tell the truths in your heart.

Sunami Publishing
Venice California

ALSO BY BRET CARR

Powdered Wings
Pluck
Die Laughing

Sunami Publishing,
PO Box 581, Venice California 90294-0581.
or call 310-289-3291
Cover Design by Trevor Elliot @ Studio Digital in Los Angeles
Printed In The United States Of America

Library of Congress Cataloging-in-Publication Data
TK

ISBN 0-96451579-1-8

"...powerful enough to take me in one session, to places traditional therapy has been unable to access over many years and much work. Thanks..."
>   - David Watkinson,
>   President Main Street Multimedia
>   Santa Monica, California

"After only three hours of Debugging... I am now lucid. I feel empowered to connect my disjointed dreams into actions that can be finally realized. I feel energized to reclaim the joy of life that is now closer to being instinctually mine."
>   - Dr. Richard DeAndrea - Medical
>   Doctor / Activist -Venice, California

"Many gracious thanks for my Debugging session. You helped me unload a few pieces of baggage I didn't even know were with me, to allow me to fly with a lighter load. Better than all the talking... we just did it. I'm free from the abandonment that keeps dragging me down."
>   - Penelope Crothru - Sales -
>   Los Angeles, California

"My entire life has just shifted perspective. To be able to tap that far back and blow away the junk, well... your book has to get out there, not only so I can start working with my friends, but it's going to make a big difference. Might even create a whole new level of actor as well..."
>   - Dan Keveany - Actor - New York City

CONTENTS

**SECTIONS HAVE BEEN BOLDED SO AS TO
EXCITE YOU TO THE IMMEDIATE
TRANSFORMATIONS
POSSIBLE WITH DEBUGGING**

CONTENTS

FOREWORD
RICHARD DEANDREA, MD

May 2, 1994

Dear Bret,

      In response to your request that I write the foreword to your book, I feel that the most powerful gift I can share with your readers is that of my own experience.

      Eight years of postgraduate medical training and experience in psychiatry, psycho-social rehabilitation, general surgery, internal medicine, naturopathy, holistics, and eastern philosophies never have allowed me a method by which to feel so whole after only three hours of "Debugging."

      The simple truth is that all my education is wonderful, but illness, whether it is mental or physical (there is no difference), all begins with unresolved emotional traumas. You have streamlined a technique to relive and 'obliterate' the cumulative effects of years of negative programming which asphyxiates the natural balance and ability of the mind-body-spirit. Debugging has incinerated the root of my depression, self-doubt, and anxieties. The ashes are now simply scattering in the wind.

      I've led a life motivated by my need for accomplishment and love. Like others, I felt

constantly impeded by an ability to over-ana-
lyze instead of 'do'. Before our time together, I
analytically conceived of every action without
realizing that I did not have to. I felt and became
aware of the abuses that were imposed on my
being as a reflection of those who had imposed
them. This was the root of my limitation. Thank
you for guiding me to the origin of my fears.
Through allowing me to relive
and safely discharge the physi-
cal and mental abuses which
were the programs of my par-
ents, my life has shifted per-
spective. I am now lucid. I feel
empowered to connect my dis-
jointed dreams into actions that
can be finally realized. I feel ener-
gized to reclaim the joy of life that is now closer
to being instinctually mine.

The most compelling bit of enlightenment I
can communicate to your readers in this foreword would
be for them to quickly turn this page. Freedom
awaits!

Author's Note:

WELCOME TO THE MOST EMPOWERING STEP FORWARD IN YOUR LIFE

Dear Reader,

You might ask yourself, right off the bat, how much of this manual can be what it claims. I'd like to take a selfish moment out to remind myself, and perhaps educate you, as to the nature of "instinct" (It is always right), and at the same time, answer your question.

Let's get complicated for only this moment. I first began my journey towards the fulfillment of human potential and enlightenment with the desire to tell stories. An instinctual need caused by a natural desire to materialize the dramas playing out in my mind. Those dramas having been etched into my circuitry by fearfully programmed parents and a society whose similarly haunted pasts have mutually brought me to my knees. As an incest survivor, convicted felon, and a scavenging addict, I have been blessed with great challenges for growth! However, more on that later.

Along the way, I was "lucky"[1] enough to find a teacher in a gentleman named Quinn Redeker who is an Academy Award nominee for writing the original DEER HUNTER story. Through Quinn and his dedication to Joseph Campbell, the mythologist, I learned that the reason stories ring emotionally true is that all humans follow, instinctually, the journey of mythological heroes. Those interpretations of Christ, Rocky, and Luke Skywalker alike, that take place in our everyday lives. Some call to adventure, signals us to an inner journey. One that we are reluctant to face. But, then, fate steps in and throws us no other choice. So, we then meet a new set of allies and enemies whom are reflections of ourselves. Then we are set to confront the deepest of our own fears, in the face of the enemy, only to come out of it with new tools to resurrect our lives and share with those that we shall love. And so, instinct is patterning and truth as we know it; ingrained in our spirits, minds, and hearts, through ages of ourselves and our ancestors repeatedly taking this same universal journey; imprinted on our cellular memory and our ge-

---

[1] Lucky - an ability to be present and available to circumstances attracted through similar conciousness.

---

netic makeup, it speaks to us in silent whispers and rapid heartbeats. This book brings us back to our instincts that, in one form or another, we pattern ourselves not to act on. We began the wheel of life in perfection. We can get back to that joyful state.

From the time I first became interested in story, I can remember my life taking on a third eye. Following my own adventure with some innate capricious knowledge that these are the destinies I can't avoid. Daily births, deaths, and resurrections. So, instead of fighting them, I guess I have hurried them along. Saying, "Come at me, and make me grow. Kill me or I shall grow stronger". I no longer have to grow through this methodology for I now have a foundation from which to flourish, rather than setting myself up for lessons learned through adversity. I now look at life not as a series of blessings and curses, but as a constant challenge for growth, with the knowledge that even tragedies are simply covert opportunities. So, perhaps my greatest adventure can now be inside of myself. Towards the heaven I have already touched on earth.

I've written this book in hopes you can join me someday.

A DAY IN THIS
LIFE WE SHARE

A Debugging
Anecdote
To Light The Way

All of my younger adult years (0-28), I used to dream that my life was one big test. Literally. Up until the time I was about fourteen, when I then sublimated this fantasy and simply continued to behave through this filter of the past, without remembering it's dramatic label. When I'd lay down to sleep at night, I'd imagine, with a hopeful knowledge that it would come to pass, that upon arrival at school the next day, the homeroom would be dark, and that all of a sudden, parents teachers and friends that I didn't know were on my side, would jump out and yell...

"Surprise, Bret! You passed the test! You are in the club. The club of life! Of sharing! Of happiness! Of love! Of acceptance... to our little whispers." ...And to the silence of their unshared laughter; and the passing smiles reserved for the safety of their little clique. And then all of a sudden I would belong.

I imagine I sucked this idea into the vortex of my mind and made it my motivation in life, hoping for the discovery of belonging. I eventually discovered, in my circular trip to that destination so close far away, that the acceptance was to be found within. And the pain I felt was the combined fear of those reflections around me.

Why just today, these visions came back to me as I walked down the boardwalk in Venice and met Jerome, the black dancing midget with no limbs and a permanent smile. If you've never seen Jerome, he is a bit of a sideshow to many passersby. Even to me until this day. His constant joy, non-stop gyrations, and hip-hop stump maneuvers are enough to make the ordinary person feel guilty about any depression they might ever have. This used to be my reaction. How can he be so damn happy? It's great, but somehow unreal. And, distant to my experience.

I was researching <u>Debug Your Brain</u>, whilst working as a Venice Beach boardwalk regressionist, on one sunny Saturday. My little stand with chairs and a sign were set up by a quiet area, facing the ocean, in front of The Fig Tree Cafe. A young man named David came to me and began by asking me to reprogram him to quit smoking.

"Why do you want me to do that?" I asked.

"Because, it costs me too much," he said.

"Close your eyes, David. What kind of cigarette do you smoke?" I asked.

I proceeded to relax him and let him sink into Alpha state. After asking him to visualize smoking a delicious generic cigarette in front of those whom he most wants respect and love from, he informed me that he couldn't imagine who that would be, since nobody has ever felt that way about him anyway. He soon admitted that he tried his third suicide attempt only the night before. This was really why he was here.

I informed David of his uniqueness and natural worth; and that he should know that whenever anyone looks into his eyes, enemy or friend, that they need him; need him for his love; need him to tell the truth about himself, so they won't be alone. Well, this was all reinforcement, though, for a stronger reality: his immediate need for a job. His life had bottomed out. And with no money, and no self esteem, he was sitting in front of me, trembling and about to implode. Through a Tarot reader friend sitting twenty yards south of me, I found him a potential job driving a gypsy cab. And, I could only hope that my affirmations sunk in and empowered him on his journey. After all, he was on a winning streak, since none of his attempts at death had worked!

As with all my weekend clients, I learn from them as well. With David, my lesson came when I told him how lucky he is that he is suicidal. That's right!

"David, you're so lucky to be challenged like this! It means that you are destined for tremendous heights in this life time. Not everybody gets to be motivated by hitting such a rock bottom. You have awareness now - and the will to change, otherwise you wouldn't be sitting here with me." After I did a thirty second finger snap Debugging, which consists of me asking him to give me an immediate response when I snap my finger and shout out the surprise association of "YOUR AGE", this twenty seven year old man answered "twelve". He answered affirmatively through a shaky voice, that, "Yes, my father molested me at that age."

I continued, "David, you are even aware of the trauma throwing you into the loop. How lucky you are to already have the monster in your grasp. Now all we have to do is re-experience it until it carries no meaning with you. You are going to be loving life. I love you for just being here with me and telling the truth about yourself. I am lucky to have a guest like you. Thank you, David, for being my friend."

Unfortunately, David wasn't available for me to continue the Debugging session with a more lengthy regression, however he was on his way to taking responsibility for his past.

So, at the end of the day, I wrapped my chair and sign up, and tucked them away in exchange for my roller blades. I skated by my "yet, never met friend", Jerome. Skidding to a halt in front of his ghetto blaster, I introduced myself to this effervescent man with two inch stumps for legs, and weird little twigs for arms which extended no more than a foot from his shoulders. His smile beamed at me through wiggly little teeth. A smile Julia Roberts could certainly have trouble competing with. Jerome, famous for his endless stump dancing, asked me how I made out for my afternoon's work. He reassured me that I was doing well, when I relayed to him that I had made twenty dollars for the day and was especially touched because I had the pleasure of meeting David also.

David brought a deeper appreciation for the true giants, like Jerome, who before this day seemed just a touch out of my reach.

"Jerome," I announced, "I've seen you so often and yet only today have I known that we've always been friends. You're so happy, it used to scare me. Now it inspires me. I feel like I've grown today, I want to tell you what happened..." I proceeded to tell him my 'David' story and then confirmed the gift of my own expanding self-esteem, "Today, Jerome, I can truly say I love you."

"Bret", he said with his stump warmly in my hand, "You're are my friend always, stop by and say hello tomorrow, whenever that may be." Jerome and I belong to each other. As do Debuggers and the Debugged.

THIS IS YOUR CALL TO ADVENTURE

For the past decade I've been compelled to wrestle with my need to create. A natural instinct, certainly. But something has made my sometime adventure a painful journey as well. I've spent ten years in Hollywood on an uncontrollable roller coaster of highs and lows; bouncing between the welfare office, directing films for HBO and Playboy, scraping along as a struggling actor, sobbing for loves lost, bussing tables, and I even once found myself on the urine-soaked floor of the county jail, arrested for selling counterfeit bank notes - I was at the effect of everything but myself. Out of control on a wild ride trying to reach for an identity abandoned so long ago; pushed away by a past of accumulated losses.

Now, I am living my dream. My career has taken off, I am contributing to my community and I am in a new and beautiful relationship - with myself. Every moment of every day is a unique and special opportunity to love, laugh, and grow. I now live in the present. All because I have told the truth about myself, shared it with others, and have taken responsibility for my feelings and, therefore, for my past. As a result, life grows more joyful and exciting every second, as continually habituating this pattern of behavior creates a stronger me.

The compiled information presented in this book has been my answer for personal freedom. Freedom from the programming of my past.

"Just when I thought I was out, they pull me back in!" - Michael Corleone GODFATHER III

Al Pacino's character need never have uttered Mario Puzzo's immortal words, if he wasn't viewing his present through filters of his past.

Having come from a dysfunctional family categorized by alcoholism, incest, and greed, I've dedicated the foundational portion of my life to re-creating an identity not founded on material value, totally avoiding substance abuse, and geared toward "free love". When, like my paternal role model (notice the root of paternal - Pattern), I became what I most resisted most, a needy criminal (fraud) who kept attracting incest victims as girlfriends and suffered daily as a love addict, my survival instinct has reached the threshold of pain and caused a new stimulus response postulate to formulate! Endlessly devastating business, romantic, and social relationships culminated in my arrest for selling counterfeit Traveler's checks- and this was the best thing that ever happened to me - the turning point of my life - I reached rock bottom and told myself... "FIND AN

ANSWER TO CHANGING YOUR PATTERNS, BRET, OR DIE! - I cannot take it anymore!"   This book is the result of tools I've compiled which have seen me look back on my past, with a knowing smile, that all one has to do is want change, and there is a simple way.

THE WAY TO BREAK THE CYCLE: WE MUST EMBRACE OUR FEARS. THEY ARE OUR BEST FRIENDS.

"When an inner situation is not made conscious, it appears outside as Fate"

- Carl Jung

These pages show how to contact your fears and turn them into your power.

There is a war that one has to wage, and here is how to make contact with the enemy. Nothing could be simpler.

Although most people I share this with won't have had an incestuous relationship or have been convicted a felon, all of you certainly have repeated unwanted patterns in your life. While not incest or crime, they may have been similar betrayals of trust dealt you by your need to become aware. These pages have turned my life from a soap opera into a love story where I am becoming causative over my life. Letting go of all control and becoming instinctively in touch with my senses and my natural baby-like state of ecstasy. A Channel for life. Moving from instinct, in a positive and loving direction. I share these tools with you so that we can celebrate together.

POSTULATE

Humans are destined to repeat the traumas of their earliest relationships (conscious or unconscious) -as they take on the traits of the conflict's victor (whether it was them or the other who won) dramatizing it for their own use in order to survive.   Thus by replaying the drama of our early relationships, we can, we believe, change the ending to our stories and make up for our painful childhoods.   And since we are slave to our stimulus response habits, our "WILL" alone cannot EVER be strong enough to change these patterns.   However, the 'will' of an additional force outside of our own, can immediately and dramatically change our destinies. One of those forces is imagination. The other is someone trained by this book who can guide you into your past.

Notes:
write down your thoughts -
it is the first step to bringing your life present,
and out of your head. With desire tangible and on
paper, we can take right action, and
create new reality.

PREFACE

The philosophy and techniques to follow are the efforts of pioneers such as Aristotle, Sanford Meisner, Count Alfred Korzybski (early twentieth century philosopher and semantic psychiatrist), Sigmund Freud, Lee Strassberg, Joseph Campbell, Fritz Perls, Carl Jung, Franz Mezmer, and many others in the hundreds of books I have studied, lectures I have attended, and therapy sessions in which I have been both guide and explorer; all to unearth my full human potential.

These same techniques in one form or another are forming the new age / human potential movement as espoused by Tony Robbins, Lifespring, A Course in Miracles, etc. All of these philosophies are workable and have wonderfully useful tools.

However, rather than write an elaborate confidence building book with my version of the same old thing, I am bringing to you just the facts; the common denominator among all of these systems; the bottom line of all the other works I have had to journey through, only to find that they end up in the same place, but sometimes decorated with such colorful fanfare that one is apt to get lost or conversely, enjoy the writing and lose the desire to act on the message.

These are the techniques that work - everything else is padding - and, yes, some of us need padding when embarking on the daring adventure of taking control of our lives.

After we accept responsibility for our life, the wonderful phenomena occurs that we immediately have no one else to blame!

I have had no special gift except the fortunate opportunity to have been driven to such a threshold of pain that I could no longer tolerate anything less than an explosion of growth. The work you are about to discover is nothing new. I have simply personalized the research and experiences of myself and these other humanistic explorers and hopefully am making it available to you in a simplified and usable text. Let's use it together.

Exploring the nature of the Hero myth led me, of course, to a study of religion as well - Religion is passed down through the ages, through story - the oldest stories of mythology that exist. I researched myth, religion, and it's application to art, so as to come up with an answer for my own pain. And in so doing, I came up with a revelation. The single recurring common denominator, method to achieving, and successful end result of all story, drama, myth, acting, art, intellectual, professional, personal, emotional, and athletic triumph, and religion is ...exteriorization. Plainly, this means getting out of one's own way. **Removing the filters of the past through which we view "now".** Living fully in the moment. Unencumbered by past conditioning. As Fritz Perls put it, **"Losing our mind and coming to our senses".** Our senses, instincts, hearts, and natural interdependence being freed from the filters of the past, results in us celebrating the life force in others and ourselves. Our need to achieve, love, share, create, procreate, etc., is not simply to have a picket fence, a BMW in the driveway, and enjoy our children, but to achieve harmony with all that exists; To enjoy the fruits of this planet which is our heaven or our hell right here on this earth - all depending on how much we can remove the accumulated losses which provide for the sludge in our boots.

In an exhaustive study, here are the two most simple, direct, usable tools to do that. The first tool is that of creating a "CHANNEL" - others call it Regression therapy, Gestalt, etc. The work seems to have originated, in modern writing, as Abreaction therapy as coined by Freud after a visit with Franz Mezmer. The unburdening and wiping away of the "old movie loops" that run through our heads, is the net effect: Dehypnotizing us of old survival patterns.

The second tool is a simplified method

of Self Hypnotic Programming or Creative Visualization or NeuroLinguistic Conditioning or whatever you want to call it. I call it "Blueprinting".

If you are ready to open your life to unlimited possibilities and be free of the compulsive thoughts and behaviors that make your world anything less than perfect, then take the small amount of time and effort, however difficult or scary it may seem, to sit down and read this book, now. The information on these pages changed my life. If you know of any better way after a decade of research with the top people in the fields of the human potential movement, the arts, and sciences, to achieve what is possible in these pages, then please write me immediately! My address is at the back of this book. Meanwhile, read on and remember to hold on to your hats kiddies, for you are about to embark on the ride of your life. The ride that will take place every moment you are alive.

LAW OF THE FARM

Dig a hole and plant a seed. Row after row after row. No getting around the effort. Just whistle while you work.

This brief chapter is my hope to communicate that no matter what obstacles you have faced in your life, anything you desire is within your grasp. You simply must fill the form. In other words, put one foot in front of the other. Just begin the journey. When I wrote my first book, I couldn't imagine creating hundreds of pages from my scattered thoughts. However, I picked up a tape recorder and started to speak. Words came out of my mouth. I put them on paper. One page a day. Then two. Then it began to take shape and come alive. Until I was riding along with the words and they finally took over and flowed through my fingers. The only credit I take is allowing my self to surrender to the natural order of life: Pure Creative Energy. I am a creation, and in turn I create. But first we must step forward and take a single breath. A single inspiration. As we release it, we begin the adventure.

Do you think it is mildly amusing that Vice President Al Gore and Tommy Lee Jones were roommates at Harvard? No. They studied to get where they are. Fortunately for us, the data in these pages, and the ability to use it, requires no more intelligence than the ability to read it. Put some effort forth and release yourself to "hitch your wagon to a star".

This is a celebration for those who want to be liberated from the prison of their own torture. A celebration of my own awakening. A guide for artists. And those who want to be skilled at crafting a future for themselves right out of their dreams.

THE AUTHOR'S JOURNEY:

EVOLUTION OF A DEBUGGER

Many people, upon discovering that I'm just shy of thirty, ask me how I came to discover such a profound life changing tool, much less have the inspiration to research, refine, and share it. This chapter touches on the events which led to the evolution of Debugging, which is really nothing new. I have simply added some New York, cut-through-the-crap guts, to a belabored process used by some enlightened "Therapists" who enjoy watching clients empty their pocketbooks and intellectually masturbate to the resultant effects of their problems, instead of addressing the early developmental causes. Or, instead, after taking a client to an emotional trauma, the "therapist" will then attempt to have the client intellectually pamper his younger self into forgiveness. Close, but no cigar. And I don't like smoke (a destructive habit reflective of inner turmoil - read the chapter "A Tough Guy Quits Smoking").

If you desire to get on with the core of the work, don't feel it necessary to read this chapter. However, if you would like an in-depth account of my own journey back from addiction, you may pick up "Powdered Wings".

As you know from reading the preceding pages, I have had the opportunity to do a lot of growing in my life. My rock bottom occurred all at once in the spring of 1992. After having been arrested for my participation in a counterfeiting ring, I was being pursued by the authorities, the counterfeiters, and others whom you can read about in Powdered Wings. However, the synchronous realizations that I had to take responsibility for my past, occurred in the following stages:

Excerpted and Amended from Powdered Wings:

The world started spinning around me -my head reeling around outside of my skull - feeling the choking air rush in, in snorted wet spasms, into the back of my blurry eyes. Little bits of inspiration, those cool rushes of moist air, taking my attention from the nearly popping stretches of sinew that pulled at the musculature of my sobbing face. I didn't really know what was happening - as this thought started tumbling endlessly through my head, with no escape, turning round and round, "How could I be so stupid..." ...Blasts of air, and salted tears erupting in the tunnelly maze inside of my head..

...and I saw all the ... The funny thing is ... Who do I see? My... What?... MY CHILDHOOD FANTASIES? ... THE GOOD TIMES?

Oh, no. The events leading up to it... That makes sense. The events that I questioned. The events that I knew contained untruths. The ones that I did the selective overlooking for. Then, as I sat there, handcuffed to the chair, rattling the cuffs between the metal legs and my bruising wrists, just to prove this was real - I thought to myself, over and over, again, "How *could* I be so stupid?"

I think, I felt I had to prove a point to myself. Some deep dark secret I'd survived, but didn't want to admit, cause it hurt - so my ego, my cocksurity, my "I'm being the best 'Bret' I can be", needed to prove that the deep dark secret never happened. All in a feeble attempt to survive the way I originally learned how to survive when I overcame those one or two forever repeated traumas of long ago. The "secrets". The "movie loops" that play in my head, which guide me from fear.

And this was the beginning of my journey to find out what it was. What dark secret brought me to this place, that only in my tears did I know was not 'who' I wanted to be.

I had to make a case for my secret. Like any great trial attorney, I hoped to do battle with the sharpest swords of my mind. Little did I know where the search would lead. But now I know that it always is - That place in which we learned to love.

This incident was succeeded by my falling into a relationship, once again, with a reflection of myself. A young lady who also was a survivor of molestation. Our relationship, like all of my relationships up until recently, was marked by compulsive obsessive ups and downs. Fighting and fucking. Two lost souls crying out for self esteem and boundaries lost long ago by the violations of adults repeating the same pattern. So, fate, that kind film director of our internal traumas, dealt me a challenge the week before I was sentenced to probation. My girlfriend dumped me, and once again, I found myself trapped in the prison of my mind, unable to do anything about the pattern that left me convulsing tears on the floor of my empty apartment.

In the aftermath of my sentencing, nearly sui-cidal, except for my innate 'third eye' which instinctually knows that life is growth, I walked the streets of Holly-wood, both looking to run into my ex-girlfriend and, with similar anxiety, looking over my shoulder for fear of the unknown. Brooding enemies and vengeful as-sailants. And again the thoughts tumbled in my head. I've escaped jail only to be locked again into the torture chamber of my past. Need to escape from this hell... I had to find a way out... A route out of the subterranean tunnels burrow-ing new sewers only one half an inch in back of my forehead. The rats of paranoia scavenging the present from sight; gobbling the light; gobble

gobble and it's becoming dark... A slow draining dark-
ness like the fist coming out of nowhere that night not so
long ago in the middle of my lonely dance with some
strange date not likely to be seen again soon for fear she
would be next.

And I find myself reliving this event when
Louis, an accomplice to my counterfeiting journey, had
me clonked on the head by some unknown ex-con - and
I'm recalling the sounds, recalling the smoky smell, and
the loud beats and muscle memory of my head being
blown to the side... "yes..just as it had happened, I feel it,"
I tell this little Asian lady, a storefront regressionist,
amazed at the clarity of my own recall.

Her sign said, "Overcome compulsive thoughts
- embrace your fear and come face to face with your past."
Well, I'm reliving the incident for the regressionist and
she asks at the snap of her finger, to recall if there was ever
a similar episode such as this one. And I don't have to do
any thinking because the snap simulates a moment of
trauma and induces a stimulus-response mechanism
which draws not on logical memory but on emotional
memory. All consuming emotional memory. I found
myself reliving a scene from my childhood. Parakeets in
my mom's living room escaping from their cage.
And I saw the fluorescent green stripe running
down the wing of that parakeet twenty six years
ago, just like it was yesterday. I became three
years old at the snap of her finger, and I watched
the male bird flutter out of the cage, followed by
it's mate. I was in my living room with my

mother, whom I later found out was molested by her father. Now, Mom never confronted her violation and since her father financially supported her, the physical violations continued emotionally for her entire life. Mom went into hysterics that day, which was not unusual. She is a germ freak. That's what happens when you don't confront your past. Those violations that leave you feeling dirty. It manifests as a fear of germs! Or birdshit as the case may be. Anyway, she had these beautiful little birds chased around the apartment and killed. Buried in AJAX. Can you believe it?! To kill the germs. These sweet little birds. A possession of the house. Like me.

"How does this make you feel?", this regression girl asks me.

"Replaceable." I say, stammering over the realization. "Like the parakeets, my mother pretended to love." And forever more I would look desperately never to be replaceable. After successively re-enacting the scenario, I transcended my emotional perspective on this trauma from one of sob filled grief, guilt, and loss, to one of humor and empathy for the silly simplicity of what was my, and still is, my mother's unfortunate programming. Those first traumas shape us. We all have a few. Everybody should be in regression. We'd have a loving world. Gandhi said, "Don't hate the criminal. Hate the crime."

And so began my research. Unable to afford this unlicensed, old world therapist, who was practicing an art of sharing as taught by every great philosopher of every modern civilization since Aristotle,

I asked her to refer me to her source books. After six months of eighteen hour days, I traced her work back through the list of philosopher / Psychological innovators listed in the first chapter. I then began to codify the work so as that I might have friends help me, aided by an early version of this book and by my Debugging of them. As I began to watch lives, including mine, change literally before my eyes, I began to share my work with strangers, via a little stand I set up on the boardwalk in Venice Beach, California. I even ran into Louis, the counterfeiter, and Debugged him in a session which brought him full circle with his childhood abandonment issues that led to his life of crime. We are now good friends and he runs a legitimate beeper business. I can't vouch for his clientele.

It became evident that anyone who is capable of listening and asking questions without making evaluations would allow what I have come to call a "Traveler", to re-experience a developmental trauma, and thereby shift perspective on an entire life and future. Freedom from programming of the past.

For we are not who we think we are. We are who we feel.

THE FINGER SNAP

A technique whereby you can get information not otherwise available to the Traveler's conscious mind and very often not even within grabbing distance of the top layer of the unconscious. This is best demonstrated by whomever handed this to you as its affect is demonstrable of the depths of the subconscious.

After a relaxed closing of the eyes, you ask the Traveler, for example, to respond with the first number that impulsively comes to him when you next snap your finger, and then when you snap, you simultaneously say "YOUR AGE" -the Traveler will rarely respond with his chronological age but instead with his emotional age. This makes for a fine magic trick but beware because the person on whom this is performed will be often sharing secrets she/he hasn't dealt with consciously, and is therefore quite sensitive to. The age will often be an age when the Traveler was abandoned, raped, divorced, robbed, or otherwise traumatized. As you become more proficient, it is not even necessary to tell the Traveler you will be asking for a number. Simply ask in a very firm tone, directly before you snap, "Your AGE!". This helps to eliminate the joker who tries to relay that 7 or 3 is his favorite number, or that he saw the number on the street sign ten minutes ago.

Every day during my practice and research of these techniques, I see people whose lives are dramatically opened up to a greater awareness. The finger snap is always the first step I use to gauge where we are heading.

Here is a brief example which occurred on the day I am writing this section. It stands out most in my mind because I was inspired by "Larry's" joy for life:

"Larry", paralyzed from the waist down from what appeared by the scars showing through his open shirt, to be gunshot wounds, rolled up to my stand in Venice Beach. He is a kind and joyful middle-aged black man who told me he wanted to find peace, and was just coming to an awareness that he has issues from his past which he wants to deal with. I assured him that embracing our pasts as challenges, for me, is the only way to find peace...

Bret: Hi Larry, ..please concentrate on the timbre of my voice and become aware of your breath. Take a deep breath... Relax yourself and look at my finger held above your head. Move your eyes not your head...As you feel the lids become heavy... allow your eyelids to flutter gently shut -Good. Now... when I next snap my finger (I snap it crisply next to his ear) you will respond impulsively with the first Color that comes to mind. You will respond at the same moment you hear the snap. You will respond without logic. In other words, don't think -just react. Once again upon my next snap, you will respond with the first color that auditorially or visually comes into your head, even if colors are coming to you now, a new one will appear on my next snap, so please respond with the first color that comes to you upon my next snap..(I tend to be repetitive so I rarely get somebody who will resist - I SNAP MY FINGER AND COM-MAND, "SKY")

Bret: (snap!) SKY!

Larry: Green.

Bret: Upon my next snap, give me the first name that comes to you. (snap!) MOMMY!

Larry: Me.

Bret: Upon my next snap, give me the first number that comes to you. (snap!) YOUR AGE.

Larry: 33

Bret: You are wide awake and alert! The world loves you! Larry, your accident occurred when you were thirty-three, correct?

Larry: Well, that was six years ago... Yes. Thirty-Three.

Bret: What happened?

Larry: I was shot seven times... as a matter of fact when you snapped and said, "Your age", I thought of the gun....My mother died during the six days I was in a coma following that..

Bret: Wow, well it seems from your response on MOMMY that you are embracing yourself as your mother. That's beautiful, you've put her spirit to work for you.

Larry: I've believed that for a long time.

Bret: How old are you?

Larry: Thirty Nine..

Bret: Six years ago you were shot. You understand by your answer that you haven't come to terms with that, yet, correct?

Larry: I know. I'm just writing a book about it now..

Bret: That's a great way to flatten that button... you know what I mean? The fact that you saw the sky as green tells me you really have a love for living things. For life.

Larry: I do...

Bret: I love you, man...

Well, needless to say, Larry, who is making a comeback as a sit down comic, indulged me in return for the free session, by giving me pointers on my comedy routine about incest. I gave him this book (pre-completion) and asked him to let me know how his writing was coming along.

IN MOMMA'S WOMB

The following Traveler came to me as a friend. He is a fellow actor and I was excited to work with him because he is already emotionally loose.

"Dan" (his name has been changed) responded to the snap tests of Color, Mommy, and Age, with Red, Gloria, and 1.

Bret:	O.k. Dan, I imagine you want to deal with the trauma of your breakup, will you tell me about the event that has you so steamed today.
Dan:	I called my house, the house where I used to live! And this son-of-a bitch answers my phone... well, when he heard my vice he put the phone down and called Gloria. I wanted to kill him.
Bret:	Take me through the episode as it occurred,

	recall it as if it is happening right now, and be detailed.
Dan:	I could hear him shuffle off to mumble something to her in the background and it' was ...
Bret:	it is...
Dan:	it is pissing me off. (he pauses)
Bret:	Where are you?
Dan:	I'm in my bathroom.
Bret:	Describe it.
Dan:	I'm on the toilet. There is a mirror in front of me that I want to smash. I don't know why I get so mad..
Bret:	I don't want to hear what you're thinking, just take me through the scene, picking up on the sensorial details as you go along. Are you clothed? What are you doing on the toilet. What position are you in?
Dan:	I'm in my underwear and the floor is cold on my feet.
Bret:	Continue with the story.
Dan:	She comes to the phone...

(he continues with a bit of the story until I am sure he is emotionally invested in his memory)

Bret:	O.k. now I want you to answer 'Yes' or 'No' at the next snap of my finger. Is this scene emotionally reminiscent of one that occurred earlier in your life. (SNAP!)
Dan:	Yes!
Bret:	Where are you?

Dan: I just walked out on the balcony of my mom's apartment. My girlfriend is making out with another fucking guy.

Bret: How old are you?

Dan: Eighteen..

Bret: Continue..

Dan: I look at them and am disgusted with myself, so I turn around back into the party and grab a beer.

Bret: (I allow him to contact his emotional memory in this scene and then perform the same snap test on him again..)

Dan: (he goes into a convulsion and slides down in his chair and puts his hands in front of his face, behaving like a child) Oh my God, I'm drowning...water is on top of me. I see my mother leave the room..

Bret: O.k..continue..

Dan: I hear somebody else scream, and I all I can see is this water (he is behaving with the tones of voice and physicalities of an infant)

Bret: Where is your mother..

Dan: I don't know...

Bret: Who is screaming..?

Dan: I think it's her..but somebody else is there..

Bret: Where are you watching your body from?

Dan: I'm away from the tub...now..

Bret: Take me through this scene from the beginning and see what else you can contact as you go..

Dan: Oh..it's my mother who screams..she

drops me into the tub..Oh my GOD..and she leaves (he screams like a baby) ..and my sister is sitting on the sink watching...(he pauses for two minutes, his head lolling about..).. it's my father..he's just come home..

Bret: How do you know?

Dan: I'm in the living room on the rug now..and they're fighting..I can't remember any more..

Bret: What kind of carpet are you crawling on..

Dan: It's not soft, I know that?

Bret: Do you see it or do you remember it..?

Dan: I see little boxes, with tassels on the fringe that I grab onto..

Bret: Continue..

Dan: And they're arguing..I can't...

Bret: Go to the beginning and take me through...

(twenty minutes later, Dan has contacted the entire scene, but it doesn't seem to be lifting, although he has now reclaimed his body and is viewing the scene through his eyes -as a one year old - ..)

Dan: My mother ran back into the bathroom when my sister screamed that I'm drowning and she grabs me and whooshes me up into her arms and she starts apologizing...

Bret: Be her..

Dan: "Oh Danny boy, my sweet sweet Danny boy -you're mother has lost her head -I'm so sorry"...she is toweling me off and she brings me into the living room and sets me down on the rug..My father is there with..another woman ...dad is dressed really nice..Mom is yelling at him, "You're no good, you're drunk...I'm sitting here taking care of the kids you no good drunk and you're running around with cheap whores".. And then my father raises his hand to her and she screams, "Go ahead and hit me you angry bum...You no good bum.." Get out..

Bret: Did you cheat on the girlfriend you currently broke up with?

Dan: Yeah, I did...

Bret: O.k., continue with the story..

Dan:..well, then my father slams the door five times and leaves with this girl...

Bret: Do you know who she is?

Dan: No?

(because he is not transcending the grief of this circuit, I ask him if there is a prior scene in his life with the same emtional content. I have him go there at my snap)

Dan:Oh my..I'm sitting in front of my Grandfather's finger, he's waving it at her telling her something in German... dubist un..

Bret: Where are you?

Dan: (He does something I haven't seen before - he places his palm in front of his stomach and curls up- "wow", I think to myself -he's in his mother's womb.)

Bret: How old are you, Dan?

Dan: Three months..

(his emotions totally sublimate his shock at having a memory from within his mother's womb, but I still see the expression of surprise. Just for my own purposes I bark out several questions asking for immediate responses.)

Bret: What year is it?

Dan: (immediate response) Sixty-five..

Bret: Where are you..?

Dan: In the study..

Bret: What do you see..

Dan: A big old radio next to my grandfather's rocking chair... And a bookcase..the carpet is dark..green..and dark curtains hang from the ceiling..

Bret: continue with what your Grandfather is saying.. Be him...

Dan: (he speaks in German) You're no good. You're no good, leaving with a sailor..a drinking   bum...and my mom is crying...

Bret: Be her and respond..

Dan: (he starts to really cry and fight back in

German. I'm able to get a brief translation
of "I love him, dadda")

Bret: Is your Grandfather drinking..

Dan: Mother Mary...he is...

Bret: O.k. Dan when I snap my finger I
          want you to answer me yes or no
          ..have you become your Grandfa-
          ther? (Snap!)

Dan: YES!(his body goes into a severe convul-
          sion and he screams - I have a nervous
          moment, but know that I must be calm)
          Yes! Oh my God Bret, the holy ghost just
          shot through me...

Bret: You've had a revelation..?

Dan: I've become my Grandfather..?

Bret: Start the scene over and go through it.

(He goes through the scene about twenty times which
takes about an hour - and finally we get to a point where
he has stopped crying and is getting irritated with me)

Dan: I don't want to do this anymore.

Bret: Good. Go to the beginning and go through
          it again.

Dan: Why?

Bret: Because it is part of the process..

Dan: But I see the fucking connection, it's been
          unbelievable - I'm getting sick of seeing
          what I've come from..

Bret: Good, you will continue. Please begin again.
          Now.

(Dan goes through it for another twenty minutes and

moves from irritation to sarcasm to laughter about it.)

Dan: I feel empathy for these poor souls...for myself..must I go through it again..

Bret: Not if you feel you're at peace with it..

Dan: I'll go through it again.

(Dan goes through the scene two more times and is left with a joyful sense of calm about what he is communicating to me - and to himself)

Bret: O.k., when I count from one to ten you will come to present and be wide awake and more alert than ever before! 1, 2, 3-10, (snap!)

Dan: Whew!

Bret: Feel good, ha?!

Dan: Man, that's gonna save me from ever having to go through that again. I don't even want to drink anymore. I understand it, Bret.

Bret: Emotionally..

Dan: Yes. Thanks man.

Bret: Thank You..

BASICS

Basic principals to know: These may seem simple, but it is necessary to articulate them now in order to lead up to later conclusions. And actions.

Man's purpose is to flourish in as abundant a manner as possible, so that, philosophically, he can reach back toward his divine nature. We don't have to travel that far however, as we are concerned with making *this* life a powerful 'moment to moment' experience. So therefore, our first order of business is to survive simply to get to that next moment. If one were to look at the irrational actions of some humans from the perspective that their behavior is a reflection of how they first learned how to survivea similar situation, then human behavior would quickly become the most predictable of one time 'mysteries'.

Everybody is born with a clean slate. An

unprogrammed computer called a brain, which formulates and builds programs via sensory input, to control the body - all in order to survive best as possible.

In our spirit's quest to come closer to our natural instincts, we are confronted with situations, including our "Karmic" selection of parents which put us into "effect" instead of at "cause", and we are subject to conflict. The conflicts we are subject to, bring us to a state where we know we must do something about them, years later, and set the wheel in motion to correct the ingrained patterns which are less than truthful to our natural instincts.

At some point, of course, the question of Past Life Regression may occur to you. It is my experience, though not at all necessary for you to accept, that past lives are as much a part of our conscience, however, much buried and of little consequence, as are the memories and programs of our current life's past. And if these 'past' lives are simply past traumas creatively expressing themselves through the imagination, this makes them no less real for the person experiencing them, and therefore are a part of his evolution. WE, MYSELF INCLUDED, MUST TAKE RESPONSIBILITY FOR CLEARING UP THE DAMAGE OF THE PAST TRAUMAS OF **THIS LIFE** BEFORE WE EVER BEGIN TO WORRY ABOUT ANY 'PAST LIVES'. THEREFORE, DO NOT BEGIN TO NEGATE THE EXTREME VALUE AND JOY YOU CAN IMMEDIATELY BEGIN TO RESURRECT IN YOUR LIFE, JUST BECAUSE I HAVE

USED THE WORD 'SPIRIT' AND IT SCARES YOU OFF. This book is a guide for all faiths and those with no faith. It is a guide which will recreate faith in yourself if it is now lost; and if indeed you are aware of our great potential no matter what our problems, it is a guide that will restore your faith in hope for all that you once wished you could help but weren't sure how. The only thing which stands between this and other similar empowering knowledge is a method for global distribution. And as enlightenment and communications is now growing in exponential proportions, we shall soon see a day when heaven on Earth will be a greater reality than we have ever known. However, given the drama that is life, the most important thing we can do is be the best we can be now. Let us take care of ourselves. Starting now. And every moment thereafter.

THEORY
OF
THE METHOD

The idea is to take ourselves and make our 'push-buttons' (those things that set us off) go from losses to wins. By perceiving them as experiences. We do this by living through them. It's easy. Just take it one step at a time...

Every first week acting student finds that we have total data available to us of every incident that ever happened. Including incidents in which we were unconscious.

Unconscious is a relative term, here. Meaning during a knockout, the fighter's mind is still recording all sounds and sensory imagery around him -except sight. However, "unconscious" also means the slight shutting down of the person and the equal and opposite take over by a the stimulus-response section of the brain which now makes a new program to create a survival pattern for the next time the fighter sees a fist coming toward him. Or for that matter, a little girl hears her drunk father slam the front door shut. She becomes unconscious and her new program built on successive old programs, or losses, causes her to shut down consciousness, like a fuse box, and go alternate -i.e.: duck her head and smile. Her endocrine system reacting by pumping adrenaline and going into apathy or placation depending on her formula created by a series of previous circumstances.

By reliving these moments sensorially. Recalling them using sight, sound, etc., we are able to experience them over and over until we are desensitized to their absurdity, and in fact they become laughable. Hard to believe but true. And it won't take you more than an hour or two of effort to experience this for yourself.

Since all our loss experiences are cyclical, this eliminates the need for us to do a Debugging exercise on every trauma we've ever had. We only need to address the one's that have the earliest programming cycles imprinted on them.

The eventual goal is to remove the past traumas which form the stimulus - response portion of our subconscious which operates out of fear. By moving these stimulus response mechanisms over to the experiential side of the mind we are no longer subject to our limitedness and thus become a Channel which can use 100% of the brain. By having total recall of our lives and being able to judge our traumas with an outside perspective we then become causative instead of resultingly an effect over our environment; Unable to be restimulated into the sleepy veil of depression.

Becoming a Channel lifts depression, ends compulsions, alleviates the monotone voice of the stifled adult-child, and recreates the joy of life that was our's at birth. The analogy comes to mind of finally being able to breathe after a life long season of the flu.

In order to Regress someone we must know about what causes the origins of stimulus response networks.

A personality is a collage of other personalities. In other words we form postulates for emotional and physical survival based on Aristotelian logic. If A=B, and B=C, then A=C.

When we observe or take part in a conflict, our stimulus response center imprints the winning dramatization on it's neural network. And then we, when confronted next time with a situation which is restimulative of the one previously experienced (and or cross referenced to other restimulators which contain similar sensorial sensations) we then dramatize the stimulus response pattern which will allow us to "survive" our situation.

Secondly, the mind stores sensorially triggered stimulus response patterns in a non-judgmental, cross-referenced and indexed, manner. In other words if a child who gets beaten by his mother with her belt and in the background a faucet is running and a piece of classical music is playing and it's a rainy day, then in the future any of these sensorial triggers will affect to the degree that they are combined, a stimulus response pattern which was originally imprinted on the beaten child, in order for that child, even if it was fifty years ago, to survive. Time does not heal subconscious wounds. It only occludes them and mixes them in with other stimulus response patterns so that we are more subtly put at their effect. And such is the sole reason for a life not allowed to be it's most capable and enriched. For if we are operating out of stimulus response patterns and not out of our "WILL", then truly, what are we but robots? The regression and reliving of 'originator' stimulus-response traumas and then desensitizing them, frees us to be in control of our "WILL". And, to experience this "WILL" with the combination and force of our education and baby like ability to play, enjoy, and learn, gives us unlimited potential. I need not elaborate on a baby's ability to learn a foreign language or to CHANNEL emotion through his body and then let it go, moving on to the next moment as if it were brand new.

The stimulus response center is the same device which caused mother to beat child just as she was beaten. The victor of her early conflict SURVIVED. This same stimulus response center is what caused Attila the Hun to slaughter masses. In terror of others, his combined stimulus response patterns, whatever they may have been, caused him to choose destruction to survive. Remember Gandhi's phrase? Do not hate the criminal, hate the crime. And in this case the crime and the criminal is the STIMULUS RESPONSE CENTER.

What would happen if the mother were interfered with from dramatizing her Stimulus response survival pattern of beating her child? Well, she would be forced to act out as the loser of the original conflict where she herself was beaten. Let's say it was her father who told her "Don't you ever hide from me again you no good little brat". Well then, certainly the mother is going to formulate based on Aristotelian logic that after all she did survive that episode, and conscious "WILL" won't allow her, unless her Stimulus Response Pattern is so restimulative that she is psychotic, to beat herself, so instead, she formulates that she is "a no good little brat". Not being conscious of this memory she falls into a "mood". Those who are repressed from dramatization are often read about going into McDonalds on a shooting spree and then ending the painful Stimulus Response Pattern in their brain by taking the gun to their own head. Better, perhaps, to regress, relive, reduce the experience, and get rid of the originating Stimulus Response Pattern.

Perhaps it's easiest to think of the Stimulus Response Patterns as "Loops" like the old dime store movies that played over and over again. Similarly, these Loops are always running in our subconscious just waiting to be triggered into stimulus response action. A circuit waiting to be activated and unleash a monster of prior survival. Sounds scary? It is!

Debugging the stimulus response center of it's negatively programmed survival "Loops" frees the poor depressed nine-to -five soul to laugh empathetically at the frustration of his co-workers; frees us to envision new futures and have the courage to make them a reality; it frees us to learn faster, create from our newly inspired imaginations and inspires us to dream of greater goals; it sets the mother beating her child free to nurture the behavior in her child that is really triggered by only her own "fear". All of this without drugging the brain with Lithium or Prozac or some other archaically murderous weapon of profit for some pharmaceutical giant.

Now, let's discuss where we might find the originators of our stimulus response patterns. MOST SRPs (Stimulus Response Patterns) are the result of traumas which occurred in the first year of life. This includes life in the womb. Life in the womb and without, at every stage of development, records 100% of auditory information. Therefore any traumas experienced in the womb and after birth, before language is understood, lie semantically, emotionally, and physically ready to be triggered.

This may be a point of divergence wherein you may say - I don't know about this?! Let me assure you that I have seen it work in regression. I can give you names and numbers of people I have guided in regression back to the womb. They have auditorially recorded everything occurring in fights between their mother and father; and the same applies in the case of children outside of the womb - they have complete sensory recall of everything at every age past conception: Sight, touch, temperature, smell, motion, pain, emotion, and of course sound. These are the senses you must be familiar with in order to guide somebody back.

Now, when a child in the womb hears his first set of dramatizations coupled with any trauma -his stimulus response survival neural network forms. Remember, he semantically records the spoken word of his parents and it is stored on his hard disk (brain) ready to be interpreted when he develops language.

So, for example, when the fetus feels pumping his mother during intercourse and hears along with it, the Mother, "Don't stop, honey", and the Father, "I want to keep going, but my I can't take it."... then, without going into complication, there you have the death of Jim Fix (Famous Marathoner who died while running). Or perhaps if that is a silly example how about a young man who strives for compulsive marathon study sessions and yet gets a migraine headache the moment he is tired. (the headache resulting from the pounding of the father into the fetus)

As science has proved, the endocrine system (glands -pituitary, thyroid, etc.) is controlled by emotional states and thus by SRPs. Therefore by removing fear based SRPs, the body rebalances and a myriad of illnesses simply cease to exist.

It is not until recently that I have remembered the severe migraines and stomach problems I had as a child. Why did it have to take so long for me to realize it was a reaction to my mothers alcoholic psychosis? Now you may say, sure, he was in pain because of how his mother behaved and in reaction to his environment, but I doubt if it was semantics exposed to him in the womb! My friend, this is where the cycle of life starts. Chances are that your environment was no different then, than it was for years after. And this is the iceberg that controls the tip of your conscious. So easy to rebalance and flush with this method.

Contacting these past traumas may seem like a job for the experienced professional. Worries of psychotic breaks may dance in your head, especially at the thought of using this pamphlet's techniques with two untrained friends. Yes, you will tap into violent emotions, watching the Traveler go through mental and physically re-triggered hysterics at times. However, at no time is he not conscious and no matter how much a session is maligned, the Traveler is better off dealing with his traumas directly than having them control him like a drug in his everyday world. Once a trauma has been confronted, the very essence of it's awareness is cause for the conscious "WILL" to begin dismantling it's push-button patterns. In such a situation where a Traveler has not ascended the emotional scale in full spectrum, the Traveler shall very much be disturbed for a day or two until his conscience has resettled. Therefore, never let a Traveler talk you out of making him stay put until he has squirmed all the way through enough recountings to shift his trauma to the last bastion of experiential memory o.that of laughter and joy -our natural state of being . You will notice that the farther a Traveler has to go (the more in grief he is when he first experiences his past trauma), the more towards ecstasy he will be when relieved of this hidden demon. It is best not to work with anyone whom is not a willing Traveler, anyway. Help those who want to change. The rest will force themselves to surface in their own due time.

There are a small group of womb semantics. Each group of womb semantics presents it's own stimulus response situation which creates behavior in later life. The most difficult of these womb semantics are those which prevent the Traveler from recalling traumas in the womb or later. We both know people who have had such severe traumas that entire patches of their existence are blocked from memory. With <u>Debug Your Brain</u> and a willing Traveler, all moments of time can be perfectly accessed through what actors call "Affective Memories", Shrinks call "Hypnotic Regression", and what I prefer to call "Traveling" - a conscious trip back in a relaxed state of mind. Anybody can do it the first time out. The chapter <u>Initiating A Regression</u> provides a step by step approach to relaxing your Traveler's brain cycles into Alpha state and then guiding him to his earliest traumas.

Reliving The Emptiness: Curing An Overeater And Ending A Lifelong Depression

DO NOT READ THIS SECTION WITHOUT HAVING FIRST READ **IN MOMMA'S WOMB -END-ING DAN'S ABUSIVE ROMANCE,** AND **THE FIN-GER SNAP.** THIS IS NOT THE FULL REGRESSION, AS THIS BOOK IS NOT MEANT TO ENTERTAIN, BUT TO EDUCATE. THEREFORE, FAMILIARIZE YOURSELF WITH THE PROCESS OF DEBUGGING AND ACCESS-ING PAST TRAUMAS BY READING THE BOLDED SECTIONS FIRST, AND THEN, FOR THOSE OF YOU WHO CANNOT ENVISION THE TIE IN BETWEEN DEBUGGING AND OVEREATING, THE SPECIFICS OF THE LOGIC, AS SEEN FROM THIS SESSION ARE ED-ITED IN BELOW.

Janice came to me knowing up front that she was molested at twelve (she thought), and although she had been in therapy for years, she was unable to overcome the programming, the robbery of self esteem, the big hole that caused her to both eat, and indulge in a wildly raunchy comedic personality, all resulting from her uncles fondling of her at eleven. Janice is a part time comedy writer / real estate broker. At the end of this session and in follow up, her humor is just as wonderful but with a greater sense of self respect attached, she is actually funnier. I find myself cheering her on as a hero instead of relating uncomfortably to her pain. (I have her close her eyes so that they flutter shut)

Bret: Color (snap)
Janice: Blue
Bret: Daddy (snap)
Janice: George
Bret: Age
Janice: 11
Bret: Where are you?
Janice: Living room
Bret: Take me to the moment of trauma
Janice: My uncle George and I were...
Bret: Are...
Janice: My uncle George and I are on the couch
           watching TV. , he was...

(after many recountings working up to her uncle's fondling her, I am finally able to have Janice relive the incident in present tense, and eventually she views the scenario from within her body. I notice that she is not emotionally connected to the trauma she describes, so I ask her to take me to a similar scene - via the snap question)

Janice: I'm in my bedroom, in this cabin we have in the country, and the walls are paper thin. My mother and her new husband are outside talking about George. I can't hear them.

(I don't give much credence to the fact that Janice thinks she can't hear what they're saying, so I ground her in the sensory perceptions of the scene and then ask her to role play her mother and father)

Bret: Is it hot in your room?

Janice: I'm crying and sweating, but I'm tucked under the blanket cause I don't want no one to hear me.

Bret: What's the temperature?

Janice: I guess it's o.k.

Bret: What does the blanket smell like?

Janice: I don't remember, um I think it smells like flannel..

Bret: Do you smell it?

Janice: No, but..

Bret: Don't stretch for it, if it's real it'll be there. Be your mother and tell me what she says.

Janice: I don't remember...

Bret: When I count from three to one, you will be your mother and recall what she says...three, two, one... (snap)

Janice: Well, something about...

Bret: Be her!

Janice: George is having problems.

Bret: Keep going...

Janice: He's impotent...

(as I finally work her into role playing her mother and father, I find that she has recalled the entire conversation)

Bret: Janice, I want you to be your mother in her full force and effect.

Janice: He can't give it to her, he's impotent, and there marriage is falling apart... (Janice begins to cry)

Bret: How do you feel about that?

Janice: Like it's my fault...

Bret: Cry, let it out, that's good, yes. Now reiterate how it makes you feel.

Janice: Dead inside, like I did something horrible, guilty, oh so fucking guilty...

(knowing that shifting perspectives on this scene won't matter as compared to lessening the effect of her actual violation by Uncle George, I decide to try and get her to be as emotional about her violation as she is about the guilty after effects)

Bret: Take me back to the living room... and go through it.

Janice: We tried it, though, I'm feeling something here...

Bret: Go back please...

Janice: O.k., I'm on the couch and we're lying next...

Bret: (interrupting) Take me right to his hand going on your leg.

Janice: He take his hand and puts it inside of my underpants and I get turned on, and then he takes my hand and puts it on his penis...

Bret: Now, slow down. How do feel about that...

Janice: Scared shitless, I knew it was wrong...

Bret: Why do you eat...

Janice: Cause I'm alone...

Bret: Why are you scared shitless...

Janice: Cause I know it's wrong and I never touched..

Bret: Why do you eat...

Janice: Cause I don't want to be alone...

Bret: Are you scared to be alone with George...

Janice: Yes...

Bret: Why are you scared shitless...

Janice: Cause I'm alone (she starts crying for the first time while reliving this scene)

Bret: Make the conclusion

Janice: ...cause I'm alone, and when I tell my mother she doesn't do anything... and I've never told anybody else... and I eat because I'm all alone... and everything I do for everybody never gets returned and I want to fill myself up.

Bret: You do everything for everybody but yourself...

Janice: That is not true...

Bret: Have you confronted your uncle George?

Janice: I don't talk to him.

Bret: Does he have kids?

Janice: Yes, I don't want to cause them pain...

Bret: See, you don't take responsibility for your

past because you think it's gonna hurt someone else. You're really worried about yourself, aren't you. Still running away.

Janice: I don't want to hurt his kids.

Bret: What? You think you're special? You think he molested you and not his little girls? I don't even have to know them to know they exhibit the same depressive character traits you have told me you suffer.

Janice: You are right... What am I going to do...?

Bret: Only you can answer that, but taking responsibility means breaking the silence. Because, the incest is not over until the silence is broken. And the emptiness you fill in by eating can only be partially removed by reliving it till the burden is removed from you. There are still victims being hurt. Every moment one of your uncle's little girls lives alone with the terror of him, a part of you dies also. And needs to eat. Eat to survive. To not feel the terror of being alone.

Janice and I spent another two hours that day reliving the moment of trauma until she became very angry with me that I kept making her relive the scene. After I assured her it is part of the process, she soon found herself laughing at the whole event and the fact that she got angry with me. She gave me a big hug afterwards.

However, I felt uncomfortable doing so, because I wanted her to own her emotions. This is my problem.

My follow up with Janice has revealed that she wrote a long letter to the eldest daughter of her uncle who now has shut himself off from the rest of the family. The 32 year old daughter is now trying to have custody of her fourteen and eight year old sisters taken away from the father. Janice tells me that some members of the family are upset with her, accusing her of projecting her own problems, but according to Janice, "...they're bums anyway, and I've never felt more alive than I do now. A part of me that was dead has been set free. That thing you wrote about, about death setting in from accumulated relationships unresolved, well -Bret, it's the best part of your book (Powdered Wings). I feel like the weight of the world has been lifted from my shoulders.

AT THE TIME THIS WENT TO PRESS, IT HAS BEEN THREE MONTHS SINCE JANICE'S SESSION. SHE HAS LOST 30 LB's. WITHOUT A DIET!

WOMB SEMANTICS

(Def: Language constructions adopted by a baby or fetus, causing him, upon language development, to subconsciously organize behavior learned through moments of trauma, according to the semantics associated with the trauma)

THIS IS THE MOST IMPORTANT AND DIFFICULT ITEM OF THERAPY PAY ATTENTION

A good Guide for the Traveler must be an investigator also. When a Loop is contacted, the Traveler will be speaking directly out of a semantic content of the conflict. The guide must pay attention to and write down semantic clues which will retard the Traveler's progress.

For example, if the Traveler says to you that he "can't go back any further", " I can't handle this right now" simply make him say that phrase again, because this will contact an EARLIER LOOP which after REITER-ATING the catch phrase of that Loop, will become accessible to the Traveler's conscious mind. THEN, IF HE IS NOT ABLE TO ASCEND THROUGH THE EMOTIONAL SCALE AND EVAPORATE THE CURRENT LOOP, YOU TAKE HIM BACK TO THE LOOP WHICH HAS JUST BEEN CONTACTED. ALWAYS BE A GOOD GUIDE BY ALLOWING THE TRAVELER TIME TO WORK THROUGH HIS TIME SHIFT. Much yawning and dopey looking head movements may occur as negative energy, moments of unconsciousness and pain, are ascending through the layers of the subconscious so that they may surface and evaporate by going over it so many times that it becomes laughable and is thus desensitized.

WOMB SEMANTICS

Travel Retarders - "Get out", "Stay away", "I don't ever want to see you again", "Shut up", "You're full of shit", "I can't go", "Don't you dare move" = this command received by fetus or child, again, is literally interpreted. It will hold him in his "flashback file" (the semantic representation of all memory assuming it is filed according to age) and not allow him, lest he be punished similarly to the loser in the original conflict, to access earlier episodes. Of course when he grows older and dramatizes the causation of this SRP, it will end in an ambivalent struggle against his instinct (conscience) and his programming - resulting in what would appear to be a 'moron' who can't properly decide for himself.

"I'm not going to deal with this", "I doubt it", "Don't you dare say a word, or else", etc. = the literal interpretation -this semantic command jams "Loops" together.

Now is a good time to clarify that memories should be classified as those items which are positive and are usable to the conscious mind as opposed to causations of SRPs which are not memories so to speak, but are in fact painful unconscious episodes which I refer to as "loops" or "scenarios."

"Forget it" - taken literally by the SRP center.

Then there was the one used on me all the time - "Take it back" - my mother was superstitious.

Listen for these phrases and similar ones that you feel are being repeated out of a moment of trauma. These are the phrases that will hamper a Traveler from regressing. The power of the phrases will be discharged by reiterating the phrase and trying to access the moment of trauma by bringing the loop present. For example: After catching on to the fact that your Traveler is speaking out of the semantic content of a trauma, have him repeat the phrase or word until he is immersed in the associated emotion. You can enhance this by having him play the role of whomever it was that you think may have said it to the Traveler. When the Traveler is fully immersed, perform a finger snap on her / him, asking, "is this loop emotionally comparable to an earlier loop, Yes or No?!" (Snap)

Remember the REITERATION trick opens up periods of unconsciousness by taking the charge off of phrases thus allowing an earlier past trauma, of which it is a part of, to be accessed. ALWAYS TRY TO GUIDE THE TRAVELER TO THE **EARLIEST** INCIDENT.

The reiteration trick can be further refined by using whatever may seem to be the common denominator of the phrase. In other words pick the active verb of the phrase and make the Traveler reiterate it, with the same feeling as the first time he said it. This way, all cross referenced Loops may be shuffled through in attempt to get the earliest, hopefully pre-natal, one.

BEING A GOOD GUIDE DOES NOT MEAN INTERRUPTING THE TRAVELER OR TALKING AT ALL, FOR THAT MATTER, EXCEPT TO GUIDE HIM BACK AND PROMPT HIM ALONG, ASKING FOR SENSORIAL INFORMATION ALONG THE WAY. NEVER EVALUATE FOR THE TRAVELER. BE A POLITE GUIDE. And always stay on top of your Traveler. But, keep your EGO out of his way while hounding him for more. AND NEVER GET SHAKEN UP. IF YOU'RE NERVOUS, SO WILL THE TRAVELER BE

TIME TRAVEL

An amazing tribute to the perfection of the mind's computer is the ability for the Guide to request the Traveler to take specific jumps in time forward or back in order to access a particular portion of a loop. It works! By minutes, days, or years.

If you bark out "what day is it?", more often that not, a Traveler recalling a scene early in his childhood, even in the womb, will, if he knew what day it was then, be able to tell you now. So, if you are rummaging around a scene and feel the Traveler is wasting time and not getting to the moment of Trauma, snap him forward five or ten minutes and dance around until you find the problem.

INITIATING
A
REGRESSION

THESE ARE THE STEPS FOR A GUIDE TO PLACE A TRAVELER INTO HIS PAST:

1.   Make the Traveler feel comfortable by letting him know that he is fully in control, and you are only acting as a guide. Inform him he will <u>always</u> be in control, awake, and although it is best for him to ask you to take him to the PRESENT he may exit the session at any time. A favorite comment that slipped out of my mouth one day was, "You are on a journey here for yourself. The farther you travel the more coal you will unearth, and then miraculously find out you are really carrying diamonds".

       Have Traveler sit comfortably but erect, answer expressively so that you can hear everything, and never let the Traveler lie down. He WILL fall asleep.

2.   Have the Traveler fixate on your raised finger, so that his eyes are lightly straining to look up from under the top of the Traveler's brow. Have him allow his eyelids to shut under their own weight. Repeat this until you see his eyelids flutter -meaning he is closing them out of relaxation instead of muscular control. The flutter with the eyes at a point behind the lids, sends a signal to the brain which simulates sleep and thus the entry into an ALPHA state where the subconscious can be accessed. Usually, the more you see REM (rapid eye movement) behind the lid, the more accessible is the Traveler to going deep into his emotional memory.

3.   Ask the Traveler to contact a moment of trauma in his past. Encourage him to pick a juicy one that occurred early in his life.

4.   Ask Traveler, "Take yourself to the beginning of that scene and tell me what happens as you go."

5.   This step is repeated over and over with the addition of, "..and pick up whatever additional detail and dialogue you can".

6.   Prompt Traveler with questions about sensory perceptions. Listen for Womb Semantics. Retarders and otherwise. And use the reiteration technique to go ever earlier and loosen up moments not available to the conscious mind.

7.   If the Traveler is not ascending up the emo-
tional scale, ask him, using a snap of the finger, if this
incident is reminiscent to one that happened
earlier. "When I count from five to one (count-
downs are useful if the Traveler is emotionally
blocked -it focuses his concentration) and snap
my fingers, answer my question with a yes or a
no", "5,4,3,2,1, is this loop emotionally compa-
rable to one that happened earlier. Snap." If yes
take him to the beginning of that scene. If no,
then be assured that a Womb Semantic is at work
and/ or that another Loop is occluding and
strengthening a block of the earlier incident.
This is where the Guide must know the terrain of
the jungle. Be brave but don't hack at the weeds. Simply
help the Traveler shove them aside. And be as stern as
you are able. IT IS IMPORTANT TO BE STERN SO THAT
THE TRAVELER FEELS GUIDED> This last item is so
important.

8.   After successfully Debugging a circuit,
bring the Traveler to present time. Give him a
countup. "When I count from one to three and
snap my finger you will come to present time".
Allow him to open his eyes. And affirm for him,
"You are fully in control of your life and in the
present. Enjoy it by making a commitment to
taking responsibility for your dreams!"

It is obviously a learned but simple process to apply this. My suggestion is to contact someone who has experienced this with either myself or an experienced Guide. Then you will have a feel for the dynamic effect that unburdening old loops can immediately have on your life.

I am so confident that this works, that upon someone's denial that this process cannot work, If they are willing to be taped for my TV pilot, I will give $1000 of my time in the form of one session to any doubter who sincerely believes he can't be helped. If at the end of one session, he is not totally convinced that help is only a desire away, then there is no charge. Otherwise the fee applies.

In addition, I provide a guarantee to be able to condition anyone in one sitting of breaking any habit they want to break. I look forward to hearing from you.

OBLITERATING A LIFETIME OF A DOCTOR'S DEPRESSION, WORRY, AND LACK OF CONFIDENCE

The following Debugging session is transcribed in full. Dig your heels into this one because it shows the investigative work required to be a successful guide. As you read through this transformation of a man, absorb the techniques you have read about. Be sure to note the simple, human, yet disciplined manner in which Debugging is successfully delivered.

Dr. Richard DeAndrea made his introduction to me on a weekend in Venice beach while mutual friends and I were playing guitar and singing impromptu political humor. He showed an interest in being Debugged and this was the result (as transcribed from a session held in his apartment on a following evening):

Bret: Richard, sit up, allright follow my hand up
           - take a deep breath... check it out -   can
           you keep your eyes on my hand?

Richard: (motions yes)

Bret: Will you do such?   You're looking at me!
           I want you to follow my finger - my wiggly
           finger with your eyes - you looking at it?!
           Good! Take a deep breath... and let them all
           fall - your eyes and your breath, together.
           There you go -great.   Allright, you're
           such a good patient.   Are you com-
           municating with me? Tell me your
           name.

Richard: Richard

Bret: Richard? Okay, good. Richard, I think we
           already know where you are. Can you take
           me back to that moment? You are on the
           stoops outside...

Richard: On the stairs outside...

Bret: actually, can we recreate our first snap test
           for the purposes of this tape?

Richard: (he mumbles "yes")

Bret: Okay, so Richard what is the negative pat-
           tern you keep repeating in your life?

Richard: Lack of confidence. Worry.

Bret: Okay, great, so when I next snap my finger,
           I want you to give me the first color that
           comes to you. (snap) SKY!

Richard: Blue

Bret: First name (snap) Mommy!

Richard: Daddy

Bret: First number (snap) Your Age!

Richard: Four

(I am surprised by this because I expected him to go to the seven year old trauma which he first told me about when I snap tested him outside.)

Bret: Okay, where are we at four?

Richard: A room. A bedroom. There are beds...

Bret: (interrupting) Take me to the moment of trauma (loud clap of my hands)

Richard: hitting...

    I interrupt to ask his girlfriend for quiet.

Bret: Go back...hitting...

Richard: Just a lot of yelling, jumping on beds. My father comes in and uh...picks up a fishing rod in the corner. A regular means of discipline.

Bret: Okay.

Richard: Just yelling. Can't understand much of the yelling.

Bret: He's yelling?

Richard: Yes.

Bret: Be him.

Richard: I don't understand why you're yelling so much. Children just don't understand.

Bret: Okay, I want you to be him again in the full force and effect that he carries.

Richard: It's really difficult. I've spent so much of my life not...wanting to...

Bret: Forget that...do it.
Richard: (he speaks without emotion) You're miserable.
Bret: Again
Richard: (angrier)You're miserable and you're rotten.
Bret: Again, be him.
Richard   (trying for emotion) You're miserable and you're rotten.
Bret: I don't believe it. Give it the full force that he does it with.
Richard: (now truly angry and loud)Would you shut up for once! Can't you be quiet!
Bret: Again.
Richard: Stop moving around. Go to sleep.
Bret: The full force and effect.
Richard: What's wrong with you.
Bret: Good. Take me to the moment of trauma now.
Richard: Just a lot of sounds of whipping, like hitting
Bret: Against?
Richard: me, my sister.
Bret: Uh, hm. Where are you watching yourself from.
Richard: From where he is. I'm in the corner. I'm hiding.
Bret: So you're seeing this scene from his point of view.
Richard: Running and hiding, pulling anything

around me I can. And he's hitting, scraping along the wall...as it gets closer it stings...

Bret: (interrupting)   Okay, as I next snap my finger, I would like an answer 'yes' or 'no'. Is this emotionally similar to an earlier scenario? (snap)

Richard: No

Bret: Okay, good. Proceed along with the scene.

Richard: Just more hitting and then a brief stop when I'm not looking, and then I hear my sister screaming.

Bret: Um, hm. Be her.

Richard: (weakly)Ow, stop.

Bret: No. Be her.

Richard: Stop, it hurts. It hurts. She's more like making whimpering sounds...

Bret: Do it.

Richard: (he whimpers for several seconds)

Bret: Take me forward. How does it resolve?

Richard: Both of us crying.

Bret: Um, hm.

Richard: For a long time.

Bret: Um, hm.

Richard: too afraid to talk to each other.

Bret: but I hear her up there. Not moving.

Richard: And then?

Bret: He's gone.

Richard: fall asleep..the corner.

Bret: Um, hm.

Richard: Thinking about why (starts crying) I didn't do anything wrong.

Bret: Good. Cry. Good.

Richard: (fighting his cry)

Bret: Give me a 'yes' or a 'no' when I snap my finger. Similar to an earlier scenario? (snap).

Richard: No.

Bret: Okay. Take me ten minutes forward (snap)

Richard: I don't understand him. I don't even know him. (crying) I don't even know why she likes him.

Bret: Do we see him again this night.

Richard: (shakes his head like a little boy)

Bret: Okay. Take me back to the point where he's whipping and yelling.

Richard: (through labored breaths) I don't understand why.

Bret: Okay take me back to the beginning of the scenario, and from the point where he's yelling I want you to be him again with the full force and effect with which
he talks to you. Right now, please.

Richard: (in his father's role) What is your problem? Just shut up!

Bret: Again.

Richard   Just shut up.

Bret: Again.

Richard: (meaner) Just shut up. Go to sleep. And...

Bret: Again.

Richard   (louder) Just go to sleep.

Bret: Again.

Richard: SHUT UP!

Bret: Again.

Richard: (louder and meaner and with good emotion - he's feeling it now) Just go to sleep!

Bret: Again, Richard.

Richard: Just shut up and go to sleep! What's wrong with you!

Bret: Again.

Richard: And just hitting and whipping

Bret: Okay, I want you to go through it again and pick up whatever additional dialogue you hear.

Richard: I don't hear anything else.

Bret: That's okay. Just go through the loop again.

Richard: I don't hear anything.

Bret: Say that.. "I don't hear anything"

Richard: I don't hear anything.

Bret: Again.

Richard: I don't hear anything.

Bret: "Shut up...."

Richard: (doesn't respond)

Bret: Please say that.

Richard: Shut up.

Bret: Again.

Richard: Shut up.

Bret: Again

Richard: Shut up

Bret: Again

Richard: What's wrong with you.

Bret: Again

Richard: Why don't you stop

Bret: That's what I want to hear. Is that him saying that?

Richard: That's me.

Bret: Oh.

Richard: (pleading) Just stop.

Bret: Good. Okay when I count from five to one (to focus him) I want you to answer my question with a   'yes' or a 'no.' (quite forceful) Is this emotionally similar to an earlier scenario? (Loud handclap)

Richard:No

Bret: Let it come... what do you see.

Richard: Ummm...hiding under a bed.

Bret: Give me a number (clap)

Richard: Three.

Bret: Who's there?

Richard: My mother

Bret: Who else

Richard: Tony

Bret: Who's that

Richard: My father

Bret: The guy with the fishing rod?

Richard: No.

Bret: Take me to the moment of trauma

Richard: She's yelling. He's hitting her.

Bret: Um, hm. Be her.

Richard: I hate you. (crying)

Bret: The same as she was
Richard: I hate you so much. (Convulsing tears) All
           you do is lie. I never see you anymore. I
           never know where you are. I never see you
           anymore.
Bret: Proceed.
Richard: He pushed her. (sniffling) They're fighting
           and I can't do anything. I can't hear her
           voice. I can only hear her cry and pushing.
Bret: Um, hm.
Richard: (cries)
Bret: Proceed
Richard: I can (unintelligible on tape) see her
Bret: What do you see?
Richard: He's punching her. He hit her in the face.
           She's trying to scratch him. She's grabbing
           him and he's leaving. She's crying with her
           head down on the table.
Bret: How does this scene end up?
Richard: She asks me if I want to take a bath.
Bret: Be her.
Richard: She uncovers the sink
Bret: Um, hm. Be her and ask yourself.
Richard: Do you want to take a bath, honey?
Bret: And you answer...
Richard   Yes.
Bret: Next. What happens.
Richard: Get in the sink and play. She just washes
           my back. (gets lost in his head)
Bret: No more trauma for that episode?

Richard: (no)

Bret: Okay when I count from four to one I want you to answer my question. 4,3,2,1 emotionally similar to an earlier scenario?

(clap)

Richard: No.

Bret: Okay, I want you to take me back to her screaming and I want you to be your mom.

Richard: Tony, I don't understand you. What's wrong with you. I love you. I don't see you anymore. Where have you been? She's hitting him. (he cries) Tell me her name. He doesn't say anything. He never says anything.

(I make him repeat this three times)

Bret: Emotionally similar to an earlier scenario?

Richard: No.

Bret: Go back and be your mother. (clap)

Richard: (in tears) Tell me where you've been. Tell me her name. Why don't you love me. She starts pushing him

Bret: And then.

Richard: He doesn't have any emotion. (convulsing tears) He's so wrong. He doesn't care about anything. Just doesn't... Nothing bothers him. He's just standing there.

Bret: Does he hit her yet?

Richard: No.

Bret: Take me through that.

Richard: Pushes him first, off. Then she comes back.

And tries to scratch him. She goes to hit him
in the face. And he looks at her, and
then he punches her.

Bret: Tell me about that.

Richard: I think he punched her in the face. He's left
handed. He pushed her and punched her.

Bret: Where are you watching this from?

Richard: Under the bed.

Bret: Where are you.

Richard: In the living room. It's a fold out bed.

Bret: And where is three year old Richard.

Richard: Under the bed.

Bret: Good. You're in your body. Go back
to the living room and be your
mother.

Richard: Crying a lot.

Bret: I want to hear what she says. Be her. In her
full force and effect, Richard.

Richard: What's the matter with you..

Bret: I can't hear you.

Richard: Why don't you love...

Bret: I want you to be her in her full force and
affect.

Richard: I can't

Bret: Please do it.

Richard: (20 second pause -practically whispering) I
don't feel close enough.

Bret: Too

Richard: Her

Bret: (rough)Good. I want you to go back to the

beginning right now and be her.

Richard:(crying)What's the matter with you. Where have you been? I love you. She's just hitting him.

Bret: Good.

Richard: Why don' you...And crying.

Bret: Don't interrupt. I want to hear what she says. Why don't you what?

Richard: Why don't you love me. What have I done wrong.

Bret: (stern)Continue being your mother please. Until she's finished. Right now.

Richard: She is finished.

Bret: Go back to the beginning right now and be her again please.

Richard: Where have you been? Tony, where have you been. I'm home all alone. What about your son. What do you think your son is going to be? You're never here. Do you care? (cries) He doesn't care.

Bret: How do you feel about that? Give me a word.(Clap)

Richard: Jaded.

Bret: How does the way 3 year old Richard feel about himself, affect the way you do today, Richard. Word(clap)

Richard: Wrong.

Bret: Go back and be your mother again, please. Right now , Richard.

Richard: It's so hard.

Bret: Good.

Richard: (bursts into tears) You just don't care. He doesn't care. What have I done wrong? What have I done to make you hate me? What have I done wrong? Tony, I hate you. I hate you so much.

Bret: Good, Richard. Keep going.

Richard: I hate you. You just don't care. Where have you been? What's her name? Tell me her name. Tell me her name. (being Tony)I don't understand why names are so important.

Bret: What are you seeing, Christian? Are you seeing something new?

Richard: He's talking but I can't hear him. He's getting ready to push her.

Bret: It's okay. I want you to go back to the beginning and be your mother again.

Richard: (no response)

Bret: Okay, I want you to listen to me. Is this event emotionally similar to a prior scenario? Yes or no, Richard(clap)

Richard: No.(he says 'No' argumentatively that I think he's hiding something)

Bret: Take a moment.

Richard: Yes?

Bret: No need to question yourself, just think of the first image (clap). How old are you?

Richard: Three.

Bret: Where are you.

Richard: Under the bed.
Bret: Okay take me back to the beginning and go through it again.
Richard: Tony I want to know where you've been. Tell me where you've been.
Bret: Proceed, Richard.
Richard: I can't hear anything. I can't get connected.
Bret: That's okay. How do you feel about me making you repeat this?
Richard: It's so hard, I'm tired.
Bret: Um, hm. How do you feel about me making you repeat this? (I'm looking for signs of annoyance or anger at the process -the first sign that the trauma is losing power)
Richard: It hurts.
Bret: Okay, good. I want you to go back to the beginning. And I want you, Richard, sit up. Sit up and take a deep breath. Okay, I want you to be your mother again Richard, in the full force and affect. In her full force and affect. Do it right, now, please.
Richard: I can't do it again.
Bret: Well, I want you to go back and I want you to go back when you hear her crying and screaming and I want you to start talking to Tony right now, please.
Richard: Who are you. I don't even know who you are. You don't work.
Bret: Is she speaking this softly to Tony.
Richard: (no answer on tape)

Bret: Okay, I want you to invest yourself fully in her emotional state.

Richard: Who are you?

(He's losing energy)

Bret: Press on, Richard.

Richard: I can't get there.

Bret: You're already there.

(then I realize that he may be talking out of a womb semantic.) Repeat that, "I can't get there"

Richard: I can't get there.

Bret: Again.

Richard: (louder) I can't get there.

Bret: Convince me of it.

Richard:I can't get there.

Bret: Okay, when I clap my hands (I get very stern) I want you to tell me if this event is emotionally similar to any event that happened previously in this life. (clap)

Richard: Yes.

Bret: Where are you?

Richard: Crib.

Bret: Um, hm. (I let him dwell for a minute) Who's there with you, Richard?

Richard: No one.

Bret: How old are you?

Richard: One.

Bret: What are you wearing?

Richard: A hat.

Bret: A hat? A bonnet?

Richard: A bonnet.

Bret: What color is it?
Richard: Blue and white.
Bret: What's the temperature in there, Richard?
Richard: It's warm.
Bret: Who are you looking at?
Richard: Myself.
Bret: Who's in the house with you?
Richard: My mother. My sister. She's wearing glasses, she looks like a cat.
Bret: Who else is there?
Richard: My mother.
Bret: Good. I want you to take me to the moment of trauma (clap).
Richard:(twenty second pause) Floating.
Bret: In that scene? Or are you floating away.
Richard: Everything is black.
Bret: Give me a number.
Richard: number? I can't think of a number.
Bret: That's okay. Who are you right now?(clap)
Richard: (no answer)
Bret: Okay. You float around now for a little while and when you contact something you let me know. I'm going to stretch.
(I take a minute break)
Bret: What do you see now, Richard?
Richard: (no response)
Bret: Pardon me for asking but what are the last words that sent us back to this point?.
Richard: I can't...
Bret: I don't connect? Is that what you said to me.

Richard: I can't connect.

Bret: Will you say that again.

Richard: I can't connect.

Bret: Convince me of it.

Richard: I can't connect.

Bret: I want you to be your mother again in the living room when you were three under the bed, again. Can you do that for me.

Richard: I can't hear her anymore.

Bret: Okay, when I count to three and clap, you will be her.

Richard: (as his mother) Tony, I want to know where you've been. What's wrong.

Bret: Grab it, Richard. And push through it please.

Richard: (mumbles)

Bret: I can't hear you Richard. Do you hear her say "what about your son?"

Richard: I know she's saying that, but she's pointing towards me.

Bret: I want you to do that right now, please.

Richard: (screaming / crying) What about your son? Don't you love him?

Bret: Continue.

Richard: You don't love anything. You don't care about anybody. Nobody but yourself. Your selfish. I can't understand you.

Bret: Continue, Richard.

Richard: He's hitting her.

Bret: I want you to go back and start talking to

Tony.

Richard:What about him? What about your son? What have I done to you. You don't care about anybody.

(Richard raises his hand)

Bret:	Did he raise his hand to you?

Richard:	I'm scared.

Bret:	Take me through it again.

(Now he really loosens up and starts balling)

Richard:	I hate you. You don't care about anybody.

Bret:	Good. This is going to clear up a whole portion of your life. Go back to the beginning.

Richard:I hate you. Go ahead hit me.

Bret:	Good. Pick up all this new information.

Richard:	You think this makes you a man? Hit me. Go ahead. You're a coward. You don't love anybody. Go ahead and hit me.

Bret:	Good. Good. Continue through it. What about your son. Sit up, Richard. You're very strong and very brave. Excellent. Excellent traveler. Now travel back to the beginning and go through it again.

(Now he really takes on the personality of his mother)

Richard:	Where have you been Tony? I want to know.

Where have you been?

Bret:	Keep going

Richard:	Tell me her name, don't push me. Go ahead if that makes you a man - hit me. Tell me her name.

Bret:	Continue through it Christian
Richard:	I can't
Bret:	Go through it. Right now!
Richard:	I can't
Bret:	Right now, please. This is part of the work. You're doing excellent. And pick up whatever additional information you can.
Richard:	You don't care? You have another baby on the way and you go out and you don't come back. What do you care about?
Bret:	Continue, Richard.
Richard	She's wearing a dress.
Bret:	Who's wearing a dress?
Richard:	My mother
Bret:	Why did you choose to tell me that?
Richard:	She looks pregnant.
Bret:	Did you just pick that up just now?
Richard:	Um, hm.
Bret:	You're seeing that for the first time?! Good. What color's the dress?
Richard:	Washed out...
Bret:	Good.
Richard:	(no response)
Bret:	Good. I want you to take me back to the beginning and go through it.
Richard:	(no response)
Bret:	How do you feel about me making you do this.
Richard:	I hate it.

Bret: You do?!
Richard: (no response)
Bret: Answer the question.
Richard: I hate it.
Bret: How do you feel about ME making you do it?
Richard: (no response)
Bret: Am I annoying you?
Richard: (nods timidly)
Bret: Okay. Good. I want you to go back to the beginning and I want you to go through it again. Right now please.
Richard: (unintelligible on tape)
Bret: Be her, Richard.
Richard: Tell me where you've been. I just don't understand you. What do you want Tony. What do you want. Do you think you're a man. What kind of man are you. Tell me who she is. Of course I want to know her name.   You're a jerk.
Bret: Good! That's a new one!
Richard: You're a jerk.
Bret: Again
Richard: You're a jerk.
Bret: Say it the way she says it.
Richard: You're a jerk
Bret: BE HER!
Richard: You're a fucking jerk!
Bret: Sit up...
Richard: You don't care about her, you don't care

about him. What do you care about. He has no clothes. What about us Tony. Does she have kids too. She's Puerto Rican isn't she?

Bret: Good, you're picking up new information all the time.

Richard: I want to talk to her.

Bret: Good.

Richard: No. I can do whatever I want. Don't you dare.

Bret: Good. Is that Tony speaking.

Richard: Yeah.

Bret: Be Tony.

Richard: You don't do anything.

Bret: He's more threatening than that isn't he?

Richard: You couldn't do anything

Bret: Just like Tony does?

Richard: He's always calm.

Bret: Say that again.

Richard: He's always calm.

Bret: Did he survive these situations?

Richard: (nods yes)

Bret: He did survive them. How did he survive them?

Richard: He walks away.

Bret: He survived them calmly.

Richard: (nods yes)

Bret: How do you feel about that?

Richard (unintelligible)

Bret: I want you to go back to the beginning and contact your mother and Tony and play both roles.

Richard: I want to know her name. You don't need to know nothing. Well I'm going to find out her name. I know she's got kids too.

Bret: Continue on with the conversation...Go on with the story would you please. Be a trouper. Tell me what's going on with you.

Richard: (stomach pain) I can't

Bret: Okay, go back to the beginning.

Richard: What about him.

Bret: I'm not satisfied

Richard: (loud)What about him!

Bret: Again.

Richard: I can't

Bret: Okay, I'm going to ask you again at my clap, is this emotionally similar to an earlier incident? (clap)

Richard: No.

Bret: Okay then go through it again. You can and you will.

Richard: What about you Tony? Don't you care about your son. Your a bastard. You're a fucking jerk. You don't care about anybody. Go ahead hit me. You're not a man. Don't push me. You can't even take care of your son. I'm gonna find out who she is. I know she's that Puerto Rican. I'll find her. You don't care about anybody but yourself.

Bret: I can't hear you.

Richard: You wont find out anything.
Bret: How's he behaving?
Richard: Aloof. Calm.
Bret: He's the survivor of this isn't he?
Richard: Yes
Bret: But you're mother is also...?
Richard: Yes.
Bret: But who's the victor of this trauma? Who's victorious?
Richard: Tony. He's always the winner.
Bret: By being?
Richard: Calm
Bret: And?
Richard: Detached.
Bret: Um, hm.
Richard: And walking out.
Bret: Um, hm.
Richard: And walking out.
Bret: And how does that affect the way Richard behaves today?
Richard: I don't like arguing. I hate it. I don't understand it.
Bret: Um, hm.
Richard: (lost inside his head)
Bret: Is it better to be Tony or to show your emotions and let them channel through you?
Richard: (no response)
Bret: I'd like an instinctual answer right now, please.

Richard: It seems like it's better to be Tony. He always wins. It doesn't seem to hurt.

Bret: It hurts much greater. The natural order of life is to let emotions flow through you. I want you to go back to the beginning and be your mother.

Richard: What about him? Is he your son? Are you going to take care of him? And what about me? You don't love anybody. You just love yourself. But I want to know where you've been. Go ahead and hit me. No man hits a woman.

Bret: Take me to the point where he hits her.

Richard: (starts crying) He Slaps her. Hits her.

(Tape ends...some moments lost)

Bret: You were being Tony. I didn't hear that. He slaps her and says... what?

Richard: You don't know anything.

Bret: I want you to sit here and reiterate that with the full emotion that Tony does until I tell you to stop. And I don't want to have to ask you to repeat it. Right now. Start.

Richard: You don't know anything. You don't know anything. (softer and more emotionally full) You don't know anything.

Bret: Again.

Richard You just don't know anything.

Bret: Okay, answer my hand clap. Emotionally similar to an earlier scenario? (clap)

Richard: No.

Bret: Okay go back and role play both sides but fast forward to the resolution of the argument.

Richard: Where have you been? Listen who's going to take care of your son? Don't worry.

Bret: Go back to the beginning.

Richard: I want to know where you've been. I thought you loved me? (As Tony) I do. Why don't you come home. I just want you to know I hate you. (as Tony) So.

Bret: Back to the beginning.

Richard: I'm gonna tell her Tony. I'm going to tell her you have a son. (as Tony) She knows. (as mother) She knows? Then she's just like you. Just a fucking jerk. She slaps him.

Bret: this is the process man. It works. Do it.

Richard: I'm distracted.

Bret: Good. Then refocus. Distraction is good for just that purpose.

Richard: I can't get back.

Bret: Say that.

Richard: I can't get back.

Bret: Convince me.

Richard: Leave me the fuck alone. I can't get back.

Bret: Make me believe it.

Richard: (begging) I can't get back.

(He starts breathing heavy and tears begin)

Bret: What are you picking up, Richard. Where are you? Give me a number. (clap)

Richard: Three
Bret: Say it again, "I can't get back"
Richard: I can't get back.
Bret: Again.
Richard: I can't get back.
Bret: AGAIN
Richard: (angry) I CAN'T GET BACK.
(I know for sure that there is an earlier incident, because this scenario is not losing it's power. I try a twist on misdirecting his focus away from the "I can't get back" impediment to earlier trauma.)
Bret: Okay a I count from five to one, reiterate, "I can't get back." Five
Richard: I can't get back
Bret: Four
Richard: I can't get back
Bret: Three
Richard: I can't get back
Bret: Two
Richard: I can't get back
Bret: One
Richard: I can't get back
Bret: Take me to the earlier scene (clap)
Richard: Sitting. There's shit all over me. It's on everything. I'm holding it, it's warm. Put it on everything. I'm afraid.
Bret: What are you afraid of?
Richard: Their reaction.
Bret: How old are you?

Richard: One.
Bret: Good. Proceed
Richard: Can't understand, they're angry.
Bret: What do you hear?
Richard: Well it's all over the place. It's pretty funny.
Bret: Who say's that?
Richard: My father. It's on everything. She's mad. She's rubbing it off. He's laughing.
Bret: Is this Tony?
Richard: (nods)
Bret: Tony is your father? Okay. Is there a moment of trauma associated with this?
Richard: Startled.
Bret: Your afraid.
Richard: Um, hm.
Bret: Take me through it.
Richard: He scares me.
Bret: Does he do something to scare you?
Richard: (unintelligible) He just laughs.
Bret: Be him.
Richard: Heh, heh, heh - he shit all over himself.
Bret: How does that make you feel, Richard.
Richard: Wrong.
Bret: Well we know that's not real. Well...it's real but we know that it's not. What happens, he laughs, "he shit all over himself" - keep going
Richard: He's pointing at everything, all over the walls. My mother is scrubbing it. She's really upset.

Bret: Um, hm. Be her.

Richard: It's not funny, it's all over. It's on every-
          thing that we bought. It's on   every-
          thing new. /(as Tony) Oh stop it. We'll
          replace it. / (as mother) How? We don't
          have any money. (10 second pause)
          How? / (as Tony) All that comes out of just
          one kid?

Bret: (I laugh) Continue...

Richard: He's a mess / Well he's your son, clean it
          up. / (as himself) So, I ate it.

Bret: Um, hm. Keep going.

Richard: Spitting it out all over my face.

Bret: Doesn't taste good...

Richard: Bitter.

Bret: Continue.

Richard: ...on my diaper. Rubbing it on myself. Tak-
          ing me to the sink to the kitchen.

Bret: Is there another moment of trauma, Rich-
          ard?

Richard: Cold water. It's freezing. She's holding my
          arms really tight.

Bret: Give me a 'yes' or a 'no', is this emotionally
          similar to an earlier scenario? (clap)

Richard: No.

Bret: Okay, take me back the beginning of it..,oh
          is there any trauma forward of this?

Richard: Yeah.

Bret: Tell me. Tell me right now, please.

Richard: Just cold water, hot water. Scrub-

	bing. (pause) talking.
Bret:	Take me back to the beginning.
Richard:	There's shit everywhere.
Bret:	Um, hm. Take me to the point where your father is laughing. Is this where your most afraid?
Richard:	No.
Bret:	Where are you most afraid?
Richard	When my mother comes in. It's her reaction.
Bret:	Which is?
Richard:	(as mother) It's everywhere. /(as father, laughing) He shit all over himself.
Bret:	Okay, I want you to repeat that. Go back to your mother.
Richard:	It's everywhere. It's all over the place / (as father laughing) He shit all over himself.
Bret:	Okay, go back to that. Your mother.
Richard:	(as mother, horrified) It's everywhere. /(as himself) She looked so startled. / (as father, laughing) Clean him up, he's your kid.
Bret:	Go back be your mother.
Richard:	Can't believe it. She's just cleaning the wall behind me. Wiping everywhere. ? Eating it. Could throw it too. She grabs me by the arm and knocks me against the crib...go to the kitchen.
Bret:	Okay, I want you to go back. Go to the beginning. Her reaction.

Richard: It's everywhere. It's all over. It's on every-
thing. She goes to clean it up. / (as father,
chuckling) He's full of shit. Your k i d ,
clean him up.

Bret: Go back, be your mother.

Richard: (as mother) Well fuck you. / (as father,
threatening) Clean him up. Now.

Bret: Who said, "fuck you"? She did?

Richard: She did.

Bret: That's okay. Good. (7 second pause) Go
back to the beginning, be your mother.

Richard: It's all over, I can't believe it. It's on every-
thing. He got it on everything. / (as father)
So clean him up. / (as mother) I don't want
to clean him up. Why don't you clean him
up? / (as father) He's your kid.

Bret: Okay - go back.

Richard: It's all over. He got it on everything. He's
ruined everything. / (as father) well clean it
up. / (as mother) Why don't you clean it up.
/ (as father) He's your kid.

Bret: Go back to the beginning. How do you feel
about me making you do this?

Richard: (unintelligible)...do it.

Bret: No. How you feel about me making you do
it?

Richard: It's boring.

Bret: Yeah? Good. Go back. Go back to the begin-
ning. Do it buddy. We're getting some-
where.

(I am trying to get him to a womb trauma or at

least a severe trauma during the first year from which he can ascend the emotional scale. However I can't seem to find it. Thus I keep him investing emotionally in this scene until I discover a womb semantic which acts as a travel impeder.)

Richard: It's all over. He got it on everything. He's ruined everything. /(as father) Well clean it up. / (as mother) Why don't you clean it up. / (as father) He's your kid./(as mother) My kid? He's your kid too. /(as father) He's full of shit.

Bret: Go back to the beginning. (sing songy to energize us both) Go back to the beginning.

Richard: He got it on everything. He's ruined everything. /(as father) Well clean it up. / (as mother) Why don't you clean it up. / (as father) He's your kid./

(as mother) My kid? He's your kid too. /(as father) He's full of shit.

Bret: Good, go back to the beginning, Richard. (we're both tired and it shows) Sit up, bud. Go back, go through it.

Richard: He got it on everything. He's ruined everything. /(as father) Wellclean it up. / (as mother) Why don't you clean it up. / (as father) He's your kid./

(as mother) My kid? He's your kid too. /(as father) He's full of shit. (his head

---

begins to loll about as if he sees something new.)

Bret: What are contacting?

Richard: (no response)

Bret: Okay, go back to the beginning. GO BACK.

(We are both severely losing momentum)

Richard: He got it on everything. He's   ruined everything. /(as father) Well   clean it up. / (as mother) Why don't you clean it up. / (as father) He's your kid. / (as mother) My kid? He's your kid too. /(as   father) Shut up. /(as mother) He's your kid too. / (as father) Shut up. / (as himself) He pushed her. Can't be right. Such a jerk. (finally, we get closer to the heart of it)

Bret: Who says that?

Richard: Me.

Bret: What are you talking about?

Richard: I didn't mean for her to get hurt.

Bret: She gets hurt?

Richard: She's crying in the corner.

Bret: (unintelligible)

Richard: Your full of shit (he starts getting emotional - choking up)

Bret: Go ahead, cry.

Richard: I can't cry that way.

Bret: When did he say, "Your full of shit"?

Richard: When he pushed her.

Bret: Are locked on to her crying in the corner over there?

Richard: Yeah.

_____

Bret: How does that resolve?
Richard: She gets up and grabs me. My head hits the inside of the crib with head. It hurts.
Bret: Um, hm.
Richard: (unintelligible)
Bret: Okay, go back to the beginning and share whatever new material you find.
Richard: He got it on everything. He's   ruined everything. /(as father) Well   clean it up. / (as mother) Why don't you clean it up. / (as father) He's your kid./
(as mother) My kid? He's your kid too. /(as father) Shut up. /(as mother) He's your kid too. / (as father) Fuck you.
(notice that, slowly, he is becoming more comfortable picking up on the violence)
Bret: Go back. How do you feel about me making you do it again.
Richard: I feel done.
Bret: Yeah. Give me a word though.
Richard: Feels useless.
Bret: A word. Annoyed...useless doesn't count. Choose between bored, annoyed, frustrated.
Richard: Bored, bored. It feels like nothing's left.
Bret: Okay, one more time.
Richard: (he is chuckling a little)
Bret: Is it funny now?
Richard: Yeah.
Bret: Oh, you're being the father.
Richard: The baby.

Bret: The baby. Oh! Good.

Richard: It's all over the place. He's got shit on everything. Shit is everywhere.(as father) He's your kid./ (as mother) My kid? He's your kid too. /(as father) Shut up. /(as mother) IIe's your kid too./ (as father) Fuck you.

(I get very stern and irritated on my last attempt to bring him earlier - watch how it works!)

Bret: Okay, I want you to listen to what I'm saying, Richard. You with me? Okay. Take a deep breath. Listen to me as I count back from five to one as you become more accessible to the traumas of your past. To the cycles which cause you to be who you are today. Five, four, three, two, one. Please answer when I clap my hands with a 'yes' or 'no' - is this scenario reminiscent of anything that happened earlier including anything that may have been pre-natal? Yes or no? (clap)

Richard: Yes.

Bret: WHERE ARE YOU.

Richard: I don't know. It's black.

Bret: In the womb. Give me a number. How old are you? (clap)

Richard:Zero.

Bret: Good, what's going on.

Richard: Light and a lot of movement. The wall just moved. Scream.

Bret: Scream.

Richard: (no response)

Bret: Do it.

Richard: (high pitch - as mother) No. No. No. Noooo.

Bret: What else do you hear, Richard?

Richard: (low, mean voice) Fucking bitch.

Bret: Is this Tony, Richard?

Richard: Yeah.

Bret: Be him. Say it again.

Richard: Fucking bitch. He's hitting her again. He's got to be hitting her. It's hitting me.

Bret: Go through it.

Richard: She's just blocking everything and he's punching her. Hitting her stomach.

Bret: Ah, hah. And you feel it?

Richard   I feel the water moving, hitting me. Walls moving. Lights. All over. Round lights.

Bret: You feel the water moving. He's hitting her. She's blocking him and you feel the water moving.

Richard: Um, hm.

Bret: And she's screaming.

Richard: She's crying. I don't want to do it anymore.

Bret: Are you talking to me or her?

Richard: You.

Bret: This is incredible. You realize that, obviously. These are major breakthroughs. (tears start rolling down his face) Good, cry. Can you take me through this scenario more, please.

_____

111

Richard: I can't.

Bret: Well, let's do it. You gotta break through this.

Richard: I can't. I don't know what's going on. Everything's moving and there's sound and I don't know what it is. Very dark. I feel myself moving.

Bret: Um, hm. (I call out to Heidi because I want her to witness the power of the mind.) Watch this. / (to Richard) When I clap my hands, I want you to give me the date. (clap) What day is it?

Richard: Wednesday.

Bret: What year is it?

Richard: 1965

Bret: Good, you're clearing up an entire life right here. Take me back to the beginning and go through it.

Richard: I can't do it. (crying sobs)

Bret: Yes, you can do it. You're changing your entire life today.

Richard: (sobbing) Just hitting everywhere. Water splashing everywhere. Things moving everywhere. I just don't want to get hit. Stopped now.

(Richard crawls up into a ball like a fetus. Reliving the hitting. He is in severe pain centered around his stomach area. He utters gasps and heavy breathing and "Oh God")

Bret: What do hear, Richard?

Richard: It's over.

Bret: Take me back to the beginning.

Richard: I can't...

Bret: Yes you can. You can get rid of a whole life of pain by braving through this.

Richard: I can't. it hurts. Oh, God.

(He doubles over and breaks out into loud anguishing sobs.)

Bret: It does hurt.

(Another thirty seconds of wrenching over the couch which he has fallen onto.)

Bret: This is good. Take me back to the beginning, Richard.

Richard: No.

Bret: Take me back to the beginning, Richard.

Richard: No.

Bret: Take me back.

Richard: No.

Bret: Let's go through it again. If we're gonna get rid of this - we're gonna blow it out. Don't want to carry it around for the rest of your life.

(for thirty seconds he gags and cries and sobs and breathes and wretches in pain.)

Bret: Go back to the beginning.

(he writhes in cramp-like cries for over two minutes)

Bret: Good. A lifetime of pain.

Richard: Ohhh, God

(he gags and buckles back and forth, rocking on the couch in pain)

Bret: Your gonna be a new person.

(a minute of deep convulsive breaths to get over the pain)
    Bret: I only hope I can train one of you two to do this to me. This is so powerful. Okay, go back to the beginning.
    Richard: (in between gags he says) No.
    Bret: This is good but let's make this work for you.
(he goes into a violent reliving of the abuse)
    Bret: (I am now simply coaxing him through with positive feedback) Good. You won't be carrying this around with you anymore. That's it. You'll be able to cook much better vegetarian food now.
    Richard: (relives the hitting for another two minutes)
    Bret: Richard, answer me when I clap my hands: Is this similar to an earlier incident? (clap)
    Richard: (gasps through clenched teeth)No.
    Bret: No?
    Richard: (through gags) NO.
    Bret: Good. This is the one we've been waiting for.

This routine continued for about thirty minutes. Richard's reactions became less and less severe. Towards the end of the session I had to clap my hands to incite him back to the beginning of the trauma. This stirred him get rid of all the muscle and emotional memory of this trauma. Before my last hand clap, I asked that

Richard sit up and take several deep breaths. He had a peaceful smile on his face and when I clapped, he gave a breathy giggle of relief.

EMOTION IS ONLY RESOLVED THROUGH EMOTION, OR ITS MANIFESTATION AS DIS EASE, NEGATIVE PATTERNS, ADDICTION, COMPULSION, & DESTRUCTION

Upon counting Richard back to present, he threw himself at me and embraced me with a hug. Something I am learning to accept more graciously. I felt we had made quite a trek on this evening and was no less happy because of the fact that I now had a trained physician to attest to the power of Debugging.

Upon checking in with Richard two days later, I found that he had an argument with his girlfriend whom was not as perturbed as she was amused that he had finally expressed a release of emotion.

PART II

COMMUNICATING WITH OURSELVES

The second set of tools are communication tools -tools to communicate with yourself in order to create an environment that you can grow into.

The first step in this process is to know that what you surround yourself with, you become. Therefore while confronting our pasts and embracing it as an experience instead of a "push button trauma", will do wonders to create a "Channel" for us to operate powerfully and fully, we must now create a "Blueprint" of a future, which reality will fill in as our "destiny".

When we surround ourselves with the weaknesses of a limiting environment and a less than loving people, we allow those weaknesses to limit us also

The first step on this journey is to look at your surroundings, and if something can be done to enhance them, then do it now. Bring living things around you. Treat yourself kindly and gently and create an environment that is inspiring.

One of the most destructive forces in the world is our loyalty based on fear

We must learn to move quickly away from those who want to bring us into their "game". Those who don't make us feel special and unique. Our psyche's have no sense of humor. Stay away from those who communicate everything in terms of terror and generality, "They say..", "Everybody knows..", "My people tell me..".. These are people who live in terror of others and will bring you down too. I used to constantly attract these people into my life, until I took responsibility for everything that happens to me. It works.

WALK AWAY FROM THE POISON PERSONALITIES OF YOUR LIFE...

...and create an environment filled with positive life affirming reminders...

And learn to Balance. Eat when you're hungry. Rest when you're tired. Exercise to keep sharp. And share the truths about yourself with others. And when looking into their eyes know that they need you. So be a good listener. Don't listen to what they say, but how they say it!

BLUE PRINTING

Once again, I want to cut through the hype and get to the point.

To create a new reality, we must have a blueprint; a goal; a dream. We must see it in our minds, commit it to paper, and affirm that we deserve it. And so it shall be.

Habits are formed by neurological conditioning. Our neurological system does not know the difference between imagined incidents and those that actually occur. They both create patterns that our neurology follows. This is how actors create real emotion. They have built up the muscle of their imagination. It is also why, those actors who draw on their own childhood traumas, instead of imaginary ones, become victims of their own talent (James Dean, Marylin Monroe, etc.) To restimulate a real incident over and over is terribly destructive, though I have several actor friends, who refuse to let go of their "talent". That is their trip. I do my job by offering the work of this book to them. Create a better human being and you create a better talent. Freer to use the imagination in all it's glory.

Therefore - we must envision our dreams, and see ourselves in them. The more specific we are, the closer we can come to achieving them now! This means we must use all of our sensorial capacities to imagine. Then, when we commit to being responsible to telling the truth about what we feel, and acting on our instincts, the similar consciousness of people operating this way will begin to attract to us. And new opportunities and seemingly synchronously magical transformations will begin to appear in our lives every day.

Blueprinting can be used to break habits as well. Simply envision great PAIN with the habit you want to break. Ask your self, repeatedly, "how does this make me feel", "how does it destroy my life", and "What does this mean to me"; keep questioning yourself and dig deeper and deeper until the threshold of pain is so great that the mere thought of envisioning your bad habit will make you wretch with despair.

Then, blueprint how your life will change, and associate all of the wonders that will come your way when you quit your old pattern. See it in your minds eye. Feel it. Know it is true.

The next transcription is from such a session. However, I do not advocate quick fixes such as the one I performed here. The roots of problems must be extinguished, before any real changes can be made. In the case presented in "A Tough Guy Quits Smoking", I chose to help the gentleman as best I could, as he began as a serious disbeliever, not only in me but in himself.

A BLUE PRINTING SESSION

A Tough Guy Surrenders
&
Quits Smoking

Here is a fine example which occurred on this January Eighth, Sunday afternoon of Ninety-Four:

This Traveler rode up on his bike with a friend. He was a bit of a rough looking older man, who carried himself with a cocky demeanor. He never gave me his name, that I can remember..

I began with a snap test. Since he didn't believe in what I was doing, I allowed him to keep his eyes open. After concentrating his focus by speaking sternly and rhythmically while staring at him, I informed him that he was going to "bark" back an answer at the snap of my fingers. I told him not to bullshit me by trying to be logical, after all, a seasoned biker like him could afford to be honest and impulsive

Bret: Give me the first Color that comes to

	you upon my next snap... (snap) SKY!
Biker:	Red.
Bret:	Name.. (Snap) MOMMY!
Biker:	Dad!
Bret:	...number (Snap!) YOUR AGE!
Biker:	he mumbles aloud...four..dy
Bret:	.was that four or forty?
Biker:	Forty, I guess..
Bret:	thought I heard you say four..
Biker:	I don't know..
Bret:	Why do you want to quit smoking?
Biker:	Cause it's bad for me.
Bret:	What does that mean to you?
Biker:	Well, I work in a hospital, and I know what can happen.
Bret:	What's that..
Biker:	Well, cancer, and emphysema..
Bret:	What does that mean to you?
Biker:	No one wants to get sick.
Bret:	What would being sick mean to you?
Biker:	That I'd be in pain..
Bret:	What do you associate pain with..?
Biker:	I don't know, no one likes pain..?
Bret:	Do you have a wife?
Biker:	Divorced.
Bret:	A girl.?
Biker:	Yes.
Bret:	Love her?
Biker:	Well, we're doing o.k.
Bret:	You don't want to marry her..?

Biker: No.

Bret: Do you want a single special relationship in your life. A love relationship you can cherish and grow old together with? A love forever?

Biker: Doesn't everybody?

Bret: Down deep, yes. Do you see any correlation between the fact that you failed at your marriage and that you are in a relationship that you're not satisfied with, and the fact that you smoke.

Biker: NO.

Bret: You don't like the fact that you are not in control of your life through your smoking, correct.

Biker: It's a habit.

Bret: So are your behavior patterns that lead you to failed relationships.

Biker: O.k.

Bret: Do you understand, that even if I stop you from smoking right now, that there are causes at work much deeper which are keeping you addicted to something... whatever it may be...

Biker: O.k..

Bret: But smoking is so dangerous to the health, that we should see if we can sublimate it to something else. Replace it with the love you are so unsuccessful at keeping, the love that I'll help you improve now, also..the love for yourself.

Biker: O.k.

Bret: Envision with you eyes closed (I teach him how to go into Alpha) that you are in front of a   dream lover, someone you want to share a life with..now imagine that you have a cigarette in your hand and she is watching it come up to your mouth..Do you understand that as that cigarette gets closer to your lips that you are telling her and reminding yourself that you are a failure at relationships. And a failure at life?

Biker: O.k.

Bret: .   Smoking that cigarette is paramount to giving up hope that you can embrace whatever in your past leads to these relationships. That cigarette says, "you are doomed to a painfully lonely cycle of mediocre ups and downs. That you are once again that lonely, miserable child."

Biker: I had a great homelife.

Bret: Be honest. Your married a girl just like your mother.

Biker: No I didn't, my mother was fantastic..My wife was a drinker and well she..it didn't work out.

Bret: Where was your dad?

Biker:	He left when I was four.
Bret:	And he was a drinker who had the same personality traits as your ex-wife..?
Biker:	Yeah, that's right as a matter of fact.
Bret:	Do you remember answering my MOMMY question by saying dad?
Biker:	YES!
Bret:	You associate an abusive paternal influence even though he left you at four, with a similar partner experience; You married you're father; the love you lost and had to get back..
Biker:	What do I do about that?
Bret:	That is regression; but we're gonna quit your smoking so you don't die before you make it through therapy..
Biker:	O.k.
Bret:	Close you're eyes... I didn't say you could come out of it.
Biker:	Sorry.

I proceed to have him visualize that his bringing the cigarette to his lips was total admissal of his inability to change his life. Furthermore that anytime he would bring this cigarette to his lips that he would be that abandoned little boy whose father came home drunk every day and screamed at his mother..And that he would be lonely and mediocre and not deserve to be loved and that he would be in pain both emotionally and cancerously...I tied every possible self betrayal and indignity possible to that cigarette. And then I asked him to envision that picture slide over to the left and move into the distance becoming dimmer and dimmer, or perhaps I asked him to envision it with an X through it. I don't remember, and it's not on this transcription tape.

Bret: Now, a new bright picture appears. One of your dream lover and your new friends. The ones who give you nothing less than total support because you deserve to be treated lovingly and gently and kindly, they are sitting in front of you..And marveling at the ability you have to be 'in the moment' with them and not piss away moments of your life reminding yourself that you are a dead man; a worthless tar sucking pitiful victim of you're own weakness by smoking those Marlborough Reds.

Biker: (he stammers through a cracked voice) O.K. I see it.

Bret: More than that, you know that every time you even have the slightest urge to smoke, that it will be replaced by the knowledge that anytime anybody looks you in the eye, whether friend or enemy, that they need you. And, that with that knowledge, you will tell the truth to them about what's in your heart at that moment. And your need to smoke will be totally extinguished; And not that it needs replacing, but it will be fortified by your ability to act as a human being with all those around you THAT NEED YOU. Now, envision this dream lover and these people watching you..see them smile and their eyes light up... and see a bright light emanate from their eyes and their smiles and it beams at you..now inhale deeply and draw that light towards you.. Good..Blow out the smoke in your lungs and at the end of your exhalation you are clean and that white light surrounds you...see it..? Good!

I then go on to affirm his strength and brevity and new found control and the fact that anything that he dreams will come closer to being his as he takes more responsibility for knowing he deserves to be loved.

I add in a safety factor, that should he have a nicotine withdrawal, he is committed upon impulse to smoke, to doing ten sit ups no matter where he is or how stupid it may look. And that if it is impossible for him to do this because he is in a tux jacket at Ma Maison, that he shall write down the number 'ten' every time he is impulsed to reach for a cigarette and then he must perform the sit ups immediately upon being able to. And I tell him to report on my answering service the number of sit ups he is doing daily. I end by reminding him that his psyche has no sense of humor, and that every time he sees a cigarette and no longer needs it, he should say, "Thank you integrity for serving me."

Bret: Now imagine yourself with that cigarette again coming up to your face in front of your new self and your new love.

Biker: It disgusts me.

Bret: Tell me a truth that is in your heart right now.

Biker: I feel like crying, but I'll say thank you instead, you have a very special talent.

Bret: You did all the work, my friend. It is you who stopped yourself from smoking. It's your power. Thank you for letting me watch as your guide.

LIFE'S TWO EMOTIONS:
1. LOVE
&
2. CRIES FOR LOVE

HOW PERSPECTIVES
SHAPE OUR LIVES

How we choose to interpret situations, determines our view on life.

Living in Venice, I am constantly confronted with reflections of myself, in the manifest of eccentrics, drunks, gang members, and soul searchers, amongst whom are the ones who believe in a fear driven God that punishes. Amongst everyone one of these Travelers, is a place of good. If they are ever able to get the better of my easy side, I simply look at them as a little child. I strip away the beard, the tattoos, the alcoholic smirk and angry loud snarl, and I see the child that was deprived, disciplined, and trauma- tized so many years ago. And then I am able to react with the right amount of love and laughter, which either disarms them or cause a fuse to blow, and away they go, enlightened, with me learning a lesson about a side of myself. This is especially challenging when I am asleep at night, and I must either blow my fuse at a loud passerby or choose to listen to them and find the good. Of course, it is best to do both. Channel my emotion and find the good. And sure enough, as I take responsibility for myself, I will be in the position to move to a place of greater calm, which in turn will reflect the move I've made inside. It all begins within. And our only power is to bring our story present. Even this section was inspired by me choosing to take a late night party-goer's rudeness, and channel it into an idea for a chapter. Instead of losing sleep, I rose out of bed and am now having the opportu- nity to share this new chapter idea with you, expand the book, and prosper through creating a better world. Then, of course, I commit to making the book great, so I can afford to move!

The game is in knowing that every moment, instead of being a blessing or a curse, is an opportunity for growth. It is all in how we choose to view it.

COMMENTARY ON OTHER THERAPIES

Some of the daring therapists, will actually indulge in their own unresolved traumas or lack of education, as the case may be, by easing patients through indirect routes of emotional release. Having treated many people who have found <u>some</u> help from analysis, dreamwork, body-work, primal screams, horoscopes, etc., I have proven to myself the thesis that the only resolution to emotional trauma is the re-experiencing of that same trauma's cyclical beginnings. Meaning, if a child has been beaten his whole life, then the parent too has been beaten, as is always the case. And, therefore, there is a time when the adult child will be able to regress to having created the foundational circuitry of surviving a beating through the parents eyes. This is what must be relived until there is emotional empathy for the parent and the child, through the adult child's eyes. No amount of Reichian therapy, which consists of triggering the muscles' armature to release emotional memory, will evaporate the semantically linked, emotional traumas which build our circuits. Language was developed and this is the foundation of our patterning. Nor will auras or horoscopes or any of the screaming, dreaming, etc., cut to the chase as definitively as getting to the root of the original programming.

To the other extreme of holistic therapy involving bodywork, primal screams, dance therapy, etc., is analysis. Here is the an example of extremes being the same as their exact opposites. No amount of talking and intellectualizing about trauma, is going to rewire circuitry. Perhaps upon the approach of undesirable behavioral patterns, after analysis, a patient may be able to have an awareness and be able to consciously avoid falling into patterns, against his instincts. But, the point is to enable ourselves to not attract these situations in the first place. And that begins with a thought pattern which is free from the trauma of the past.

Then, of course, there are those who actually do regressive therapy, and are led emotionally back to early traumas. However, most Traveler's I speak with, tell me that once the "therapist" feels they have contacted the moment of trauma, they then are coddled into accepting it and letting it go through a pseudo intellectual process of forgiveness. This is fine, but again, any intellectual process that substitutes emotional understanding, will simply leave the equivalent amount of circuitry still doing it's damage.

All reality is shaped by thought. We become what we think of ourselves, as learned early on. Luck, as defined earlier, is simply being aware of situations at their moment of inception, and being 'present' enough to act upon the sincerity of those moments with a humanity that energizes both parties. Have you ever noticed that your 'lucky' friends are always the ones who don't worry, and live only in the moment, sometimes to the point where they are absent minded? This is no coincidence. They are living life, while others are making plans.

For whatever reasons it has been a mystery in the past, for the "seeker" to find answers for himself, well, it is here on these pages, now. At least with regard to the possibility of being open to the adventure that life can be.

As this is a time in history in which communication is becoming central to our evolution, we are witnessing a rebirth of spirituality and truth. I say, "Welcome to the information superhighway of our communication with ourselves."

FOR THE ACTOR
IN ALL OF US
SENSITIZING OURSELVES

Instinct and the ability to act as a channel is some-
thing that is heightened through debugging. However,
in the same manner that a muscle is built up through
continuous use, we must habituate ourselves to being
sensitive. The more people have been traumatized, the
more they are armored against being sensitive. This
armoring is apparant in their narrow emotional range,
monotone voice, and serious analytical behaviour. Some-
times, severerly traumatized people, have a difficult time
sensorially regressing. They have intellectuallized their
entire past so as not to feel the pain. Unfortunately, this
inherent curse of intelligence, produces an over-wired
thinker, afraid to be a feeling - acting human being. Cut
off from the joy of the moment, all of their senses are
filtered through the fuse box of reason. Therefore, it is
desirable, as it continues to be for me, to continuously
work out the muscle of sensitivity. I present to you on the

next two pages, a sacred excercise taught by Sanford Meisner to some of the greatest theatrical stars of our time. Practiced over a long period of time, this 'repetition technique' enlivens the natural emotional instincts dormant in everybody. Did you know this is why we are taken with actors? They are able to remove themselves from their heads, moving from spontaneous moment to next moment with the power of an open channel. Repsonsible to their heart and of equal importance, to the hearts of their partners.

When we open ourselves up to others, our space expands into theirs. Being a good listener and impulsively acting upon how we feel about what is going on in the moment, is one of the best ways I know to begin to invite new relationships.

Of course, many times it is hard to fathom how we may jump beyond our fears and into the realm of what we 'know' exists. For we do know everything about each other the moment we meet, and then we have to relearn it all.

So, I drift back to my days in 'method' acting class when we were put onto stage and had to look at each other and 'react' or 'repeat.' Meaning that the first and strongest feeling we had concerning how the other person made us feel was what we had to share - from our point of view. Even if it was, "Wow, you have great tits!", then that is what we had to share -- however, since our hearts weren't usually affected by great tits -this would have been a supreficial comment; more appropriate would be, "Wow, I am so turned on by you," to which our 'repetition' partner would have to respond by either repeating from their point of view the same words, or, respond with an observation on what they saw going on in the other person. So to say in a monotone voice, "that's vulgar" is not appropriate - it is selfish. And that is the beauty of this 'repetition game'. It enlivens us to how other people make us feel, and better than that, since we have to answer from our point of view, it forces us to feel what they are saying rather than hearing the words that they cover thier thoughts with. So, the young lady to whom I remember saying, "Wow, I am so turned on by you,"perhaps answered with, "You ARE so turned on by me," at which point I might have said, "You're surprised!" and so on... the point being to learn to react intictively from our hearts.

After about a month of daily five minute practice sessions of this 'repetition game', I witnessed transformations take place in my fellow students and myself. Tears, laughter, rage, and compassion 'channeled' through us, moment to moment, habituating us to our natural state of baby-like sensitivity; rebuilding the muscle of free emotion that had been armored against by the stifling of fearful, dysfunctional, truamatized role models who dramatized thier 'shit' on us in order to survive. Like any muscle: instinct, the imagination, and our ability to channel emotions can be built up through practice.

A warm up for the repetition technique is the 'three-moment' game. You ask your partner a provocative question, which they then repeat from their point of view, and you then respond by observing what you felt they actually meant when they repeated. For example:

Bret:	Do you think actors are vain?
Laura:	Do I **think** actors are vain?
Bret:	You think that's a rediculous question, and you know actors are vain.

Of course, the questions can reach whatever depth you are willing to plunge to. So be brave and dive in. This is an excellent tool with which to begin a 'repetition' session, as it can naturally flow into repeating and observing, and reacting to behaviour.

Perhaps if enough people read this book, it will help end the wasted energy applied by those who come to Los Angeles and figure they can wake up in the morning, decide they're attractive, take a picture and be an overnight sensation.

Like anything else in life, including clearing one's past whether through Debugging or some other method, one must build a foundation built on strong technique, specificity, and all backed up by desire; the only element truly necessary for any change.

"He who cares most, wins."
-Rosanne Barr

RECYCLABLE ABUNDANCE -
An Experiment In A New
Economic Model

Having scavenged, at times, to simply make ends meet, I have found it necessary to examine my perspectives on abundance. Growing up with the notion that knowledge and wealth are tokens to be slaved for, I was being led by the fear of a generation not prepared for the joy of giving as a reward unto itself. We cannot truly appreciate anything in this life until the joy we know is shared. Sometimes, this takes place through the kindness extended to a stranger's smile. Other times it is simply understanding that everyone operates out of a need for love, and thereby finding forgiveness where it otherwise might not exist. It is up to us to sharpen our ability to recognize opportunities. Any time anyone looks us in the eye, or a familiar face triggers our instinct, we are being called upon to celebrate attracting consciousness, by exploring what knowledge is there to be shared and grown from.

I believe that in the future, the monetary system as we know it, is going to be replaced by credits garnered for sharing enlightenment. As successive new generations are taught to revel in the bliss of life, they will reward their mentors with abundance to match the empowerment they receive.

In keeping with this idea, I'd like you to join me by sharing this work, which was channeled to me through the creative and loving energy of the universe, and thereby reap rewards of not only connecting your brothers and sisters with themselves and each other, but also by sharing in the abundance of the exchange.

Because you have already purchased this book, you are a member of an exploding community of spiritual consciousness.

If you have bought this book directly from Sunami Publishing then, the person who turned you on to these pages has shared in your good fortune in many ways. If you bought this book retail, then you may write to us and be included in this experiment in abundance - a new economic model.

Using our exchange system, as it is now, your 'mentor' (the person whom recommended the book to you) will receive a payment from the publisher of $.50 cents. When, for example, you turn "Debug Your Brain" onto two friends of your's, then you shall also receive $.50 cents per book purchased and so too, shall your 'mentor'. So, he shall have $1.50 (in addition to his .50 cent sale to you). When your two friends reciprocate this act, your 'mentor' shall have been rewarded with another $2.00 and you with $2.00. When the level of consciousness goes one deeper and your two friends' two friends, have turned the book on to two of their friends, then your 'mentor' shall receive $6.00 - by the time the level of consciousness has sunk only 6 levels deep, you will have received (assuming the example of dual turnover) $55.00 and have reached 63 people and you and your mentor will have shared in the energy of an increase spiritual consciousness and an abundance to recycle your growth.

Examine the exponential rewards of sharing and you shall see that knowledge is indeed, power.

Unlike multi-level marketing, this is not a get rich scheme. It is an experiment which does not take precedence over the empowerment possible fro using the techniques in this book. So, if you attempt to create a downline (a marketing term that means someone who solicits people to network under them in order to create income), know that every purchaser will be called to make sure this work is not being distributed for those purposes. You have power in your hands, dear reader, share it with integrity.

Be gracious and kind when demonstrating the "Finger Snap". There will be people who have come to peace in their lives through their own journey and will have no need for this information. There will, however, be a majority of people who you will open up new worlds for with the simple demonstration of where they are stuck. Many of them will actually be able to recall the trauma which occurred at their particular 'emotional age' and after whom they are patterning their life; romantically and otherwise.

As with any teaching, support and sharing are the only way to advance the cause. So, be brave. Excavate those past traumas and throw them in the garbage where they belong. Work with your friends. And prosper in the abundance of a life that shall renew itself in each moment. Bless the GODYOUARE.

SUMMATION

These are only basics - And the answers are no more complex than stated here. However, there are those of us, an old me included, who like to know everything before taking a step forward. I suggest you do both: take a step forward into action and then support that by further education.

To know without doing is not to know at all

For those of you who want more specificity on these subjects, here is a reading list of the finest and most motivational material around. These are works that brought me to where I am now:

Powdered Wings by Bret Carr, a love addict's escape from a billion dollar ghetto. I really believe in this one.

The Artists Way by Julia Cameron, a powerful workbook for creative and spiritual growth and recovery. Changed my life.

The Celestine Prophecy by James Redfield, a transformative adventure.

The Way of the Peaceful Warrior by Dan Millman, a transformative journey.

Creative Visualization by Shakti Gawain, an absorbing elaboration on how to create reality from dreams.

The Holographic Universe by Michael Talbot, a must read in order to understand the nature of the brain and it's interplay with physical reality.

ABOUT THE AUTHOR

Bret Carr is constantly trying to lose his mind in order to come to his senses. He currently lives and works in his body and travels west in order to explore the east. He spends time researching more ways to be in the moment while also connecting with this hollographic universe. If you have any suggestions, he encourages correspondence from his readers.

For More Information:

Address:
Sunami Publishing
12100 Wilshire Blvd. #770
LA, CA 90025

To Order A Copy of Powdered WIngs
Send $14.00 (this includes handling)
or
For Additional Copies of Debug Your Brain
Send $ 12.00 (this includes handling)

To Participate in the
Recylable Abundance Program,
add $10.00.